Death Records of Pioneer Missouri Women

1808-1853

by
Lois Stanley
George F. Wilson
Maryhelen Wilson

Southern Historical Press, Inc.
Greenville, South Carolina

Copyright 1990
By: Southern Historical Press, Inc.

All rights reserved. No part of this publication may be reproduced, stored in a retrieval system, transmitted in any form, posted on to the web in any form or by any means without the prior written permission of the publisher.

Please direct all correspondence and orders to:

www.southernhistoricalpress.com
or
**SOUTHERN HISTORICAL PRESS, Inc.
PO BOX 1267
375 West Broad Street
Greenville, SC   29601
southernhistoricalpress@gmail.com**

ISBN #0-88308-762-9

Printed in the United States of America

Obituaries as we know them did not exist in Missouri until late in the 1800s. But death notices began with the first newspaper, the famous old <u>Missouri Gazette</u>. Fortunately for researchers, many deaths noted were women... whose names would never appear on a census, might not be found in a marriage record.

This listing combines two earlier volumes (deaths 1808-49, 1850-53). They do not cover the whole state for the whole period, since some areas had no newspapers. But they provide many names which might otherwise be lost to research.

The first woman's death notice in a Missouri newspaper was that of "Mrs. Frances Dorr, wife of Lieut. Joseph" who died at Ft. Bellefontaine near St. Louis in 1808. Early records were brief, but as time passed they became more detailed. Notices would include the name of the husband (or late husband, in the case of widows); date of death, age, possibly number of children or former residence. The notice might add "Virginia please copy" implying a relationship with that state (or New York, or Ohio, or Kentucky, or others). A surprising number included the name of the deceased's father, though rarely the mother's. Religious denominations were often mentioned-" a Baptist for 30 years."

Deaths of infant girls are not shown here, but the listing includes <u>all</u> reported deaths of girls who would have appeared in the 1850 census; for the earlier years, records include "daughters" whose ages were not given, and girls who had reached the age of ten years.

Some of the names, of course, are those of prominent families, but they are the minority. Most of the notices are those of beloved women whose grieving relatives chose to let others know of their deaths through the newspaper. Some died very young, some lived a very long time. But all of them deserve to be remembered.

(A few of these records - 1808-16 - have appeared
in the National Genealogical Society <u>Quarterly</u>.)

```
        RECORDS FOR 1808-1849           p 1
        RECORDS FOR 1850-1853           p 81
```

NEWSPAPER CODE, CITY AND/OR COUNTY WHERE LOCATED

BEA	Beacon	St. Louis city and county
BGDB	Democrat Banner)	Bowling Green: Pike
BGRAD	Radical	
BOBS	Observer	Boonville: Cooper
BOLT	Boonslick Times	Fayette: Howard
BORE	Boonville Register	Boonville: Cooper
BRUNS	Brunswicker	Brunswick: Chariton
CAMP	Plebeian	Canton: Lewis
CANE	Northeast Missourian	"
COMB	Commercial Bulletin	Boonville: Cooper
COP	Patriot	Columbia: Boone
GLWT	Weekly Times	Glasgow: Howard
HANT	Tri-Weekly Messenger	Hannibal: Marion
FAR	Far West	Liberty: Clay
FREEP	Free Press	St. Louis city and county
FULT	Telegraph	Fulton: Callaway
INJN	Journal	Independence: Jackson
INP	Independent Patriot	Jackson: Cape Girardeau
JASO	Southern Advocate	" "
JEFRE	Republican)	
JEM	Metropolitan }	Jefferson City: Cole
JINQ	Inquirer	
KCEN	Enterprise	Kansas City: Jackson
LEXP	Express	Lexington: Lafayette
LEXA	Appeal	" "
MIN	Intelligencer	An important early newspaper published first in Franklin, then Fayette (Howard Co.) and finally in Columbia (Boone). Wide coverage.
MOAR	Argus	) St. Louis city and county
MORE	Gazette or Republican	
MODE	Democrat	Fayette: Howard
MOH	Herald (Mo. Herald)	Jackson: Cape Girardeau
MOP	Missouri Patriot	St. Charles city and county
OSIN	Independent	Osceola: St. Clair
PLAT	Argus	Platte County
PWH	Whig	Palmyra: Marion
NERA	New Era	St. Louis city and county
SALT	Salt River Journal	Bowling Green: Pike
SASE	Sentinel	Savannah: Andrew
SCOMB	Commercial Bulletin	St. Louis city and county
SLAM	American	"
SMAD	Southern Mo. Advocate	Jackson: Cape Girardeau
SLDU	Daily Union	St. Louis city and county
SOV	Shepherd of the Valley	"
SLINQ	Inquirer	"
SPAD	Advertiser	Springfield: Greene
STCHMO	Missourian	St. Charles city and county
STCWR	Weekly Republican	"
STEGPD	Plain Dealer	St. Genevieve, town and county
STGAZ	Gazette	St. Joseph: Buchanan
WAR	Visitor	Warsaw: Benton
WEM	Western Emigrant	Boonville: Cooper
WEPT	Western Pioneer	Trenton: Grundy

Most newspapers covered several surrounding counties. These listed are generally available at the Newspaper Library, State Historical Society of Missouri, Columbia. Some are at the Missouri Historical Society, Jefferson Memorial, Forest Park, St. Louis.

ABBEY, Mrs. Alpha O. died in this city (St. Louis)　　MORE 20 Aug 1833
　　　Sunday evening.

ABBOTT, Mrs. Lydia Maria died at Lynn, Mass. 21st inst.　　MORE 30 Apr 1838
　　　wife of John C. of the firm of Hood & Abbott,
　　　St. Louis & daughter of the late Aaron Breed, Esq.

ABEL, Mrs. Margaret died at West Ely 4th inst. in her　　PWH 8 Oct 1846
　　　73rd year

ABRAMS, Mary Ann wife of William H. died of bilious　　MORE 12 Apr 1835
　　　fever Sunday evening age 32. Louisville and
　　　Baltimore pc.

ADDISON, Margaret drowned from the steamboat Convoy en　　MORE 15 July 1846
　　　route from New Orleans. Her family was emigrating
　　　from England to St. Louis and she was believed
　　　to have been carrying 70 sovereigns, their entire
　　　wealth. A body believed to have been hers was found.

ADDISON, Mary E. wife of John died 26 March, late of　　MORE 31 Mar 1843
　　　Washington City. Zanesville OH & the
　　　National Inquirer pc.

AGEE, Catherine Amanda consort of Philip died 11th inst　　CAMP 27 Apr 1849
　　　in her 23rd year.

ALEXANDER, Mrs. Anne consort of Lieut. Thomas died at　　MORE 27 June 1835
　　　Jefferson Barracks 24 June.

ALEXANDER, Sarah Ann consort of B. W. died Saturday.　　SCOMB 8 Aug 1836

ALEXANDER, Mrs. Elizabeth died at Ft. Towson 31 Oct.　　MORE 5 Dec 1834
　　　wife of Lieut. F. (or E) age 28 after a
　　　long illness.

ALLEN, Ann consort of Beverly died in New Orleans on　　MORE 20 Nov 1832
　　　Thursday, 1st inst.

ALLEN, Celeste, wife of Beverley Allen Esq. died in　　MORE 26 July 1831
　　　Ste. Genevieve 21 July in the 23rd year of her
　　　age, the only child of George Bullett, Esq. of
　　　Cape Girardeau.

ALLEN, Elizabeth consort of Jedediah died in Ste.　　MORE 12 Sep 1835
　　　Genevieve 7th inst. (Mother of Beverly)

ALLEN, Marion W. consort of William died 13th inst.,　　PWH 20 Aug 1845
　　　leaving husband and several children.

ALLEN, Mary Augusta died 9th inst., wife of John A. of　　MORE 21 Nov 1845
　　　St. Louis, in Manchester, Mass.

ALLISON, Rebecca, consort of Hugh, died 25 May age 73.　　WEM 13 June 1839
　　　33 years a Baptist. Liberty MO pc.

ALTON, Mrs. --, consort of John, died at Jackson, Mo.　　SMAD 15 Sep 1838

ALVAREZ, Josephine, consort of the late Eugenio, died　　MOAR 11 Sep 1835
　　　3rd inst ae 76.

AMELIA ANN, Sister of Charity, died of cholera at the　　MORE 10 Sep 1833
　　　St. Louis Hospital yesterday evening.

1

AMSE, Rectina wife of Nathan died age 52 at her residence, 2nd above Cherry. Interred Baptist Burying Ground. — MORE 27 June 1849

ANDERSON, Mrs. -- died of cholera at Palmyra. — MORE 28 June 1833

ANDERSON, Anna Maria wife of Wm. C., Jr. and daughter of Henry L. Yeatman of Warrenton, VA died in her 30th year. Interred Wesleyan Burying Ground. — MORE 16 June 1849

ANDERSON, Nancy consort of John B. died 9th ult. in her 52nd year in Jefferson Co. Member of the 2nd Presbyterian Church, St. Louis. Interred in family burying ground near Herculaneum beside daughter Albertine Caroline who had died a few months earlier ae 21. (This cemetery apparently was identified as "Dr. Cooley's".) — MORE 13 Feb 1845

ANDERSON, Margaret J. wife of George C. and oldest daughter of John Maitland Esq. of Philadelphia died Monday afternoon age 28. Buried Philadelphia. — MORE 29 Apr 1840

ANDERSON, Mrs. Eliza M. wife of Maj. William C. died 9th inst. Funeral from her residence on 6th St. between Carr & Washington. — MORE 10 Feb 1841

ANDERSON, Nancy wife of James died on Ramsey Creek 23rd inst ae 53. Late the widow of Maj. Ambrose Buford, formerly of Bourbon Co. KY. Was a Baptist. — BGRAD 21 Oct 1843

ANDERSON, Rosalie (or Rusella), wife of Thomas L. of Palmyra, died at the home of her mother Mrs. Easton in St. Charles age 30 year 4 days. Left 2 children. — MORE 3 Dec 1840

ANDREWS, Eliza Ann wife of Ambrose died 18 Nov. age 33. Resided #88 Market St. New York pc. — MORE 20 Nov 1844

ANDREWS, Mrs. Polly, consort of Richmond, died Monday last age about 68. — MODE 18 July 1848

ARBOGAST, Ann, wife of M. (prob. Marcellus) died last night. Pittsburgh & Chillicothe OH pc. — SWERE 18 May 1849

ARCHER, Mary Ann, wife of Edward and daughter of Thomas Shore, Esq. died 4th inst age 37. Funeral from residence late Thos. Shore, 6th & Carr, to Episcopal Burying Ground. — MORE 5 Apr 1849

ARNOT, Mary Jane consort of Anderson died at Glasgow Monday week in her 25th year. — BRUNS 7 Apr 1849

ASHBY, Mrs. C. (Cassandra) died of consumption of the lungs in her 50th year. — BRUNS 8 June 1848

ASHLEY, Eliza B. consort of Gen. W. H. died Tuesday evening last. — MORE 8 June 1830

ASHLY (sic), Mrs. Mary, wife of Gen. Wm., lieut. Gov. of Mo., died in St. Louis 7th inst. — MORE 14 Nov 1821

ATCHISON, Louisa, wife of Samuel died 3rd inst ae 26. — NERA 4 Mar 1848

ATWOOD, Susan, consort of Dr. F. B. of Carrollton, died 29th
  inst in her 31st year after a "painful and   BRUNS 7 Oct 1848
  protracted illness."

ATWOOD, Mrs. died recently at Memphis, consort of Dr. N.B.   MORE 30 Sep 1828
  Atwood, formerly of St. Louis.

AUDRAIN, Mary E. relict of Col. James died 10 Dec. in   MORE 2 Jan 1835
  St. Charles Co.

AULL, Mrs. Margaret died 25 Sept. in Lexington in her   MORE 21 Oct 1836
  66th year. Many years a resident of Newcastle, Del.
  Presbyterian.

AULL, Matilda, consort of Robert, died at Independence   MORE 22 Jan 1839
  29 Dec. Daughter of Stephen Donaho, Esq., of
  Howard Co. MO.

AUSTIN, Mrs. Mary Ann, consort of William J. of   MORE 14 May 1833
  St. Louis, died Thursday.

AUSTIN, Louisiana, consort of Archibald. A., died   MORE 30 Jan 1840
  Thursday 8th inst. ae 23. Funeral from residence
  of S. Williams, 110 Main. Methodist Burying Ground.

AVIS, Mrs. Caroline H., wife of Samuel, died in her   MORE 21 Oct 1842
  36th year. Funeral from her residence, Franklin
  & 8th St. Boston & Providence RI pc.

AYRES, Lucy, wife of Col. B. W. died last evening in   MORE 7 Aug 1841
  her 65th year. Catholic Burying Ground.

BACKINSTO, Mrs. Mary died at the residence of her son   MORE 16 July 1845
  Benjamin 12th inst in her 69th year.
  Fincastle, VA pc.

BACON, Miss Maria E., formerly of Salem, Mass., died   SWERE 9 Mar 1846
  in St. Louis 5 March ae 24.

BAILEY, Susan C., consort of Col. David of Troy,   MORE 22 Sep 1835
  Lincoln Co., died in St. Louis 29 August.

BAILEY, Mrs. Mary Ann died in St. Louis Co. 23rd inst   MORE 31 Jan 1848
  ae 67.

BAILEY, Mrs. Mary E. died Saturday night last.   MORE 11 Nov 1834

BAIRD, Elizabeth, consort of William and daughter of   BGRAD 14 Sep 1844
  the late Rev. Samuel Findley died age 53 on 23 Aug
  in Louisville, Lincoln Co. Presbyterian 20 years.

BAIRD, Mrs. Judah age about 70 died near Louisville,   BGRAD 17 Feb 1844
  Lincoln Co. Thursday last.

BAIRD, Mrs. Mary died in Lincoln Co. 11th inst, consort MORE 21 Apr 1829
  of James. Left husband and an infant.

BAKER, Ann, wife of James died Friday last in her 18th   MORE 17 Feb 1849
  year. Late of Moline, Rock Island, IL.

BAKER, Mrs. Fanny, consort of Dr. C. W., daughter of   BOLT 19 Oct 1844
  Joseph Sears of this co., died at Savannah MO.

3

BAKER, Patience wife of John died in St. Louis Co. 27 March ae 42 y. 2m.   MORE 6 Apr 1840

BALCON, Armenia wife of Aaron died 29 May ae 23.   MORE 2 June 1846

BALLINGER, Levitisa consort of Elder E. Ballinger died 31 July.   PWH 13 Aug 1845

BANE, Mrs. Hartford died in Calumet Twp. Saturday age about 45.   BGRAD 27 July 1844

BARADA, Josephine Robert wife of Isadore died 15th inst in St. Joseph, MO.   MORE 25 Sep 1844

BARBEE, Mary, wife of William, merchant, died 26 March.   MORE 2 Apr 1847

BARBER, Nannie W., wife of William B., died Tuesday ae 24. (MORE adds that the funeral was from the residence of Trusten Polk. Her name is given in a legal notice as Mannie.)   SWERE 26 Nov 1848

BARNES, Mrs. Mary died 25th inst in her 53rd year. Funeral from residence of her son William, Franklin near 14th. Also mentions son Robert A.   MORE 26 June 1844

BARNES, Frances A. widow of William died at Rocheport at the residence of N. Cutler.   COMB 19 Nov 1846

BARNETT, Mrs. Elvira died 2 July ae 42. Funeral from residence of T. Barnett, Green & 7th Sts. Interred Baptist Burying Ground.   MORE 3 July 1848

BARNETT, Mary, wife of Ro. P. was killed by lightning (possibly in Lincoln Co.) on 14 June. She and George N. Wells were riding horseback to visit a sick friend; both were killed, as were both horses. R. P. was en route to California.   PWH 28 June 1849

BARNWELL, Mrs. Charlotte C. died 9 Sept. at Ft. Towson, wife of Lt. Thomas O., in her 25th year. Daughter of Lt. Col. J. H. Vose.   MORE 14 Oct 1836

BARR, Mrs. Jane S., wife of John T. of New York, died Thursday morning last age 43.   MORE 23 Jan 1841

BARRON, Sarah, consort of John, died 29th ult. in her 32nd year. Funeral from residence, 6th & Green. Catholic cemetery. Referred to as "mother."   MORE 1 Mar 1844

BARRON, Susan, consort of Charles H., died in Randolph Co. MO 29th ult in her 27th year.   BOLT 10 May 1845

BARRON, Virginia Ann, youngest daughter of Charles H., Esq. of Glasgow, died at the residence of her grandmother Mrs. Jane Cockerill of Randolph Co., MO 29th ult.   MODE 7 Nov 1848

BARROW, Mrs. George died age 38 y. 5 m. Funeral from the residence of her don-in-law John King, 228 N. 7th   MORE 14 June 1849

BARTHOLOMEW, Maria T., wife of J. W. and daughter of Theodore Byington, Esq. of Southampton, Conn. died 26th ult. age 21.   MORE 12 Feb 1844

BARTON, Izetta, consort of Kimber, died at Glasgow   BRUNS 23 Aug 1849
    15th inst in her 24th year.

BASCOM, Mrs. Margaretta, consort of Hiram B., died   MORE 26 June 1834
    Tuesday last. (SOV, 27 June, shows "Henry")

BASYE, Mrs. Ann, consort of John W., died Tuesday. She   SALT 5 June 1841
    was 64, and a Methodist.   "   7 Aug 1841

BATES, Mrs. ___ and child died of cholera in Waverly.   BRUNS 12 July 1849

BATES, Caroline Matilda died in St. Louis 15th inst. at   MORE 17 Oct 1845
    the residence of her son Edward, age 94.

BATES, Mrs. Charlotte, late consort of Moses, Esq.   MORE 1 May 1818
    died at Potosi, Washington Co.

BATES, Mrs. Eliza, relict of Joseph, age about 26.   MORE 30 Mar 1838
    Funeral from her residence on Washington Ave.
    to the Presbyterian graveyard.

BAXTER, Mrs. Mary died 3 Sept. age 24.   CAMP 8 Sep 1848

BAYLESS, Dorcas died at the residence of her son near   MORE 9 Aug 1845
    St. Louis 4th inst in her 64th year. Late of
    Fauquier Co. VA

BAYLESS, Susan, wife of William and daughter of Jonas   MORE 2 Aug 1847
    Newman died 1 Aug. Funeral from her residence
    144 Locust to Episcopal burying ground.

BEAL, Nancy wife of Benjamin died 14th inst ae 80.   SPAD 20 Aug 1844

BEATTY, Elizabeth Longdo, wife of Alexander, died   SWERE 24 Dec 1848
    yesterday age 39.

BEEBE, Mrs. Livonia, consort of William B., died in   BGRAD 2 Dec 1843
    Hannibal Monday last.

BELDEN, Mrs. Agnes W. died 29 Dec 1843 at Monticello,   BOLT 6 Jan 1844
    age 37, consort of Joshua and eldest daughter
    of Judge Lewis. Cause of death, apoplexy.
    Left husband and children.

BELL, Elizabeth, consort of John M. of Chariton, died   MIN 9 Oct 1821
    2nd inst. "wife and mother."

BELL, Mrs. Henry was killed by lightning in Clay Co.   22 June 1843 MORE
    2 June. (Husband and chuld also killed.)

BELT, Eliza M. died yesterday morning at the residence   MORE 21 May 1838
    of Mrs. H. N. Belt, age 16. Formerly of
    Winchester VA.

BENOIST, Mrs. Eliza wife of Louis A. of St. Louis   MORE 23 Aug 1827
    died at Kaskaskia 11 Aug.

BENOIST, Esther S., wife of Louis A., died 30 Aug. at   SWERE 4 Sep 1848
    the residence of James S. Thomas. Funeral from
    St. Francis Xavier Church.

BENT, Martha, relict of Silas, died Monday last.   MORE 23 Aug 1833.

BENTLY, __, consort of Samuel, died at Rocheport, Boone Co., Saturday last, formerly of Howard Co.   MODE 4 Apr 1848

BENTON, Mrs. Ann, mother of Thomas Hart Benton, died night before last at the residence of Mrs. Brant. (SMAD 2 Jan 1838 calls her relict of Jesse)   MORE 4 Jan 1838

BERKLEY, Zoe, wife of George and daughter of the late Antoine DuBreuil died 23 Feb ae 28.   SWERE 28 Feb 1848

BERRIAN, Mrs. Sarah died in St. Louis Sunday morning last, late of Brooklyn NY.   MORE 7 Oct 1834

BEST, Thirsa Jane, ae 17, daughter of Lewis M. and Rachel, died 14 May at Pleasant Grove, Livingston Co.   BRUNS 31 May 1849

BIDDLE, Ann, widow of Maj. Thomas died 10th inst. Funeral from residence of Major Harney to the Catholic cemetery.   MORE 12 Jan 1846

BILL, Mrs., consort of Charles, died Monday last.   MORE 6 Oct 1819

BILLINGSLEY, Mrs. Mary, late of Virginia, died 29 July in Cooper Co.   BOLT 10 Aug 1844

BINGHAM, Eliza, daughter of Henry V., died in Franklin Thursday last ae 17.   MIN 5 Mar 1821

BINGHAM, Sarah E., wife of George C., rep. from Saline Co., died at Arrow Rock 29 Dec. ae 29.   BRUNS 6 Jan 1849

BINGHAM, see WILLIAMS

BIRCH, Hannah, wife of Albert Sr., died at Ste. Genevieve 14th inst age 62. Native of Philadelphia.   MORE 20 Mar 1849

BISHOP, Martha J., consort of Dr. J. A. J. died 5th inst.   PWH 11 June 1842

BISHOP, Mary Ann, consort of Nimrod and daughter of Alexander Keith of Fauquier Co., VA died 21st inst in her 48th year.   COP 25 Nov 1842

BISSELL, Mrs. Debora, relict of Daniel, died 13th inst age about 78.   MORE 15 Nov 1843

BISSELL, Mrs. Mary A., consort of Capt. Lewis, died the 5th inst. in St. Louis Co.   MORE 8 Aug 1834

BLACKFORD, Mrs. M. of Boone Co. died 24 June at Fort Laramie of cholera, age 50.   MORE 7 Oct 1850

BLACKWELL, Lavina, relict of Robert, died 7 Dec 1848 at the residence of Michael Can in Washington Co. Kentucky pc.   MORE 15 Jan 1849

BLAIR, Caroline, wife of Montgomery, Esq. died in her 26th year.   MORE 12 Jan 1844

BLAKEY, Mrs. Mary, consort of Maj. William, died 23rd inst at Palmyra. Left 6 children.   SALT 6 Feb 1841

BLAKEY, Amanda, wife of John D. and daughter of A. Huntsberry of Lexington, MO died in Central Twp. ae 26 y 4m 4d.   MORE 24 June 1850

BLAND, Eliza relict of Thomas died near Bowling Green   BGRAD 3 Aug 1844
    Thursday ae 45.

BLOCK, Mrs. Delia consort of Phineas died at Louisiana,   SALT 3 Oct 1840
    MO in her 34th year. Born in Richmond VA.
    (MORE 2 Oct. says she died 29 Sep. and left
            husband and children)

BLOW, Mrs. Elizabeth consort of Peter died in St. Louis   MORE 26 July 1831
    after a long and painful illness.

BLOW, Eugenia Labeaume wife of Peter Esq. died 24 Dec.   MORE 25 Dec 1846
    Funeral from St. Xavier's Church to the
            Catholic cemetery.

BLUE, Miss Nancy Adelia, sister of Dr. John H., died   BOLT 18 Sep 1841
    17 Aug. in Chariton Co. Formerly of Thompkins
                            Co. NY

BOGGS, Miss Sarah of Putnam Co. died on the way to   BRUNS 9 Mar 1848
    Oregon in Cochran & John's Company.

BOILVIN, Mrs. Ellen, consort of Nicholas, U. S. Agent   STCHMO 1 July 1820
    at Prairie du Chien, died 19 May at the
    residence of her father near St. Louis, ae 32.

BONNVILLE, Margaret H. died at an advanced age 30 Oct.   SLDU 31 Oct 1846
    Native of France. Buried Catholic cemetery.

BOONE, Mrs. Chloe, relict of Jesse B., decd, died in   SLINQ 2 Sep 1822
    Callaway Co. 20 Aug.

BOON, Mrs. Nancy, wife of Col. William, died in   MIN 4 Apr 1835
    Fayette 24 March.

BOOTH, Mary Ellen, wife of Nathaniel, died in St.   MORE 27 Aug 1846
    Francois Co. 20th inst in her 25th year.

BOSWELL, Mrs., wife of Hartwell, Reg. of Land Office   INP 15 Nov 1823
    for the District at Batesville, Ark. died
    6th inst. "Wife and mother."

BOSWORTH, Annie Lester "last of the little choir"   SWERE 26 Aug 1844
    of Judge Felix, Louisiana, died 16th inst
    a few miles from town.

BOUIS, Mary, consort of A.R., died at the residence of   MORE 20 Oct 1838
    Robert Forsyth in St. Louis Co. Funeral from
    residence of her brother Thomas Forsyth (farm).

BOUIS, Mme. Vincent, one of the city's oldest French   5 Jan 1845 MORE
    inhabitants, died 1 January age about 77.

BOWEN, Mary Mildred wife (possibly daughter?) of Dr.   JEFRE 18 July 1835
    John W. died of cholera at Palmyra 17 June
    at the age of 16. See also WILLOCK.

BOWYERS, Mrs. William J. died at the Sulphur Springs   MORE 6 May 1843
    24 April, daughter of James Hunt Esq. of
    Trenton, NJ. New Jersey papers pc.

BOYD, Alice C., consort of the Hon. Linn of KY, died at   MORE 9 Oct 1945
    the residence of George Gordon, Lafayette Co.,
                    ae 31y 11 d.   7

BOYD, Mrs. Christopher of St. Louis died, no date shown.   MORE 13 Sep 1820

BOYD, Mrs., wife of Col. Marcus, died 15 September. She   SPAD 20 Sep 1845
left 9 children.

BRADLEY, Mrs. Mildred died yesterday in St. Louis at   MORE 24 Sep 1835
an advanced age.

BRADY, Mrs. Katherine died on Thursday last at an   MORE 17 May 1817
advanced age.

BRAGG, Mrs. __, consort of Joseph, died 13 May in her   MODE 23 May 1848
70th year.

BRANGLE, Ursula died 11 January in Palmyra.   PWH 22 Jan 1846

BRANHAM, Elizabeth Ann, wife of Dr. N. E., died 27th   FULT 15 Sep 1848
inst at the residence of her father, John
Hobson, age 30. Native of VA, she emigrated
to Missouri with her parents in 1839.

BRANSTETTER, Susan, wife of Frederick, died at Cuivre   BGRAD 21 Sep 1844
Sunday ae about 43.

BRANT, Elizabeth, wife of Capt. J. B. of the U. S.   MORE 10 Jan 1828
Army, died last Saturday.

BRAZEAUX, Mme. Maria died 27 Nove,ber.   MORE 5 Dec 1810

BRAZEAU, Widow Therese, died yesterday in St. Louis.   MORE 3 Feb 1834

BRICE, Mrs. Susan, consort of John J. of Pike Co.,   SALT 16 Jan 1841
died 6th inst. near Frankford.

BRIDGE, Isabella E., wife of Hudson E. and daughter   MORE 2 Oct 1846
of the late Nathaniel Holland of Walpole, NY
died in her 27th year. Funeral from her
residence, 8th St. near Olive.

BRIDON, Mrs. Louisa Catherine died at residence of her   MORE 25 Sep 1832
daughter 17 Sept.; formerly of Paris, France.
(BEA 20 Sep says she was the widow of Louis
Francois Bridon)

BRIGGS, Mrs. Ann E., wife of Robert of Hannibal, died   MORE 28 Mar 1838
20 March in her 17th year, leaving an infant.

BRIGGS, Darcus, wife of Caleb, died in St. Joseph   MORE 5 Sep 1850
19 August.

BRIGHT, Mrs. Adele F., consort of George Y., died near   STCHMO 15 Dec 1821
St. Louis.

BRIGHT, Mrs. E., wife of Josiah and daughter of Charles   MORE 15 Feb 1817
Sanguinet, died "yesterday in childbirth."

BROCK, Mrs. __ of Carroll Co. committed suicide last   MODE 6 Sep 1847
Tuesday by hanging.

BROOKS, Anna M., wife of William K., died 16th inst   MORE 26 Sep 1848
in Philadelphia age 47.

BROTHERTON, Mrs. Elizabeth, consort of Marshal, died   MORE 29 Nov 1837
Monday evening last.

BROTHERTON, Rebecca died in St. Louis yesterday afternoon   MORE 6 Sep 1838
    age 66. Funeral from her residence on Spruce
    St. to the Presbyterian Burying Ground.

BROWN, Adelaide, consort of Col. John of Saline, died in   BRUNS 7 Apr 1849
    her 51st year on 14 March. Formerly of Bath Co. VA

BROWN, Mary E., consort of Robert T., died 3rd inst in   MORE 18 Jan 1844
    her 24th year. Left 2 children. She was the   JINQ 18 Jan 1844
    daughter of Col. Edward M. Holden, Perryville.

BROWN, Ann E., consort of Livingston and only daughter   MODE 4 July 1848
    of John B. Clark of Howard Co., died in Albemarle
    Co. VA 6 June in her 23rd year.

BROWN, Susan I., consort of Constantine, died 11 April   PWH 23 Apr 1842
    ae 40.

BROWN, Elizabeth, consort of John, died 28 Dec 1841 in   PWH 1 Jan 1842
    her 29th year. Left 4 children. Born in
    Harrison Co. KY

BROWN, Mary widow of Moses Brown of Baltimore Co. MD   SWERE 10 Mar 1845
    and eldest daughter of the late Francis Snowden
    of Baltimore Co. died in St. Louis Co. 16 Feb.
    age 67.

BROWN, Sarah L., consort of the Rev. John R., died   31 May 1831 MORE
    Sunday morning of last week in her 32nd year.

BROWN, Mrs. ___, consort of Levin, died of cholera   MORE 28 June 1833
    in Palmyra.

BRUBAKER, Mrs. Elizabeth, wife of Abraham, died   STGAZ 24 Apr 1846
    of pulmonary consumption 18 April in her
    58th year

BRUFFEY, Damarius Elizabeth died 6th inst in her   MORE 7 Jan 1845
    11th year, only daughter of Mary D., late of
    Lewisburg, VA, and niece of S. V. and E. H.
    Farnsworth. Funeral from residence of E.H.
    72 N. 2nd to Methodist cemetery.

BRUNSON, Sarah wife of Joseph W. died in St. Louis   SWERE 30 Apr 1849
    24 April ae 28. Wheeling VA & South Bend pc.
    (MORE 26 April says Josiah)

BRYAN, Mrs. Mary E. died 25 Oct in her 24th year at   MORE 1 Nov 1837
    the residence of her father in St. Louis Co.
    Consort of Dr. Edward H. of Mississippi and
    formerly of Prince George Co. MD

BRYAN, Mary Melvina age about 12, youngest daughter   MIN 21 Dec 1833
    of Sally McClelland, died 18 December.

BRYANT, Catherine, wife of Powhatan, died in Spencer   BGRAD 30 Sep 1843
    Twp, Pike Co., 13th inst.

BRYANT, Mrs. ___, wife of Rolla, died in Paynesville   BGRAD 9 Nov 1844
    in October.

BUCHANAN, Mrs. Adeline, consort of Edward W., formerly   MORE 2 Oct 1838,
    of St. Louis, died 25 September age 19.

BUCKLIN, Mary Ann wife of James M. died in St. Louis Co. 19 Dec. in her 37th year.　　MORE 21 Dec 1848

BUCKNER, Mrs. Alexander died of cholera 7 June in Cape Girardeau Co. (Her husband also died)　　MORE 25 June 1833

BUCKNER, Mrs. Nancy consort of Stanton D. died 9 March.　　SALT 21 Mar 1841

BUERGER, Mrs. Conrad; she was murdered by John Golder and a group of "Citizens of German Descent" offered a reward for his apprehension. (He was later caught and returned to St. Louis.)　　MORE 14 Mar 1844

BURCKKARTT, Sarah, relict of Col. N. S., died in her 45th year.　　BOLT 14 Oct 1843

BURKE, Mrs. Sarah died 26 June age 63.　　SWERE 3 July 1848

BURKLOE, Mrs. Eliza consort of Samuel V. died at St. Charles in her 27th year leaving husband and 3 children. Daughter of the late John Ferry and only sister of Gen. B. Emmons Ferry of Boonville.　　BORE 14 May 1844

BURNETT, Miss Emiline died in Boone Co. 14 July.　　MORE 2 July 1844

BURNS, Jane, wife of Andrew was murdered "Wednesday last" by a Shawnee Indian called "Little George."　　MOH 19 Aug 1820

BURROWS, Margaret, wife of Col. Nathaniel died in Savannah, Andrew Co. in her 36th year. She was born in Trenton NJ, daughter of the late Arthur Curry. "Wife and mother."　　COMB 17 Feb 1848

BYNUM, Martha, only daughter of Gray, died 24 Dec 1846 in her 23rd year.　　MODE 6/4 Jan 1847

CABLE, Lucy died 11 Jan. at the residence of J. Lackland　　MORE 12 Jan 1848

CALDWELL, Margaret daughter of the late David Logan Caldwell died in Perry Co. 30 April.　　SOV 16 May 1835

CALLAWAY, Amanda Catherine consort of Charles B. died 15 Jan. age about 20 leaving an infant son.　　BORE 25 Jan 1845

CALLENDER, Mrs. Isabella, wife of William D., formerly of Boonville, died in Falmouth, Maine age 24 on 9 January.　　MORE 27 Jan 1843

CALVERT, Mrs. Frances K., consort of Sanford and late of Galena died 26 October.　　BEA 3 Nov 1831

CAMDEN, Mrs. Mary, consort of Maxwell, died yesterday. Funeral from the family residence on 8th St. near the college to the Presbyterian Burying Ground.　　MORE 1 Apr 1837

CAMDEN, Mary, widow of Micajah, died 27 Nov. in her 76th year. A Methodist for 50 years. Funeral from the residence of P. C. Camden on Broadway near the Big Mound.　　MORE 29 Nov 1847

CAMDEN, Sally T. died in her 64th year. Funeral from residence Broadway & Howard to Presbyterian Cem.　　SLAM 4 Apr 1845

CAMPBELL, Cornelia daughter of Dr. and Amelia died   SWERE 16 Feb 1846
     10 Feb. age 13 years

CAMPBELL, Emily, wife of Thomas, died 7 May ae 32.   SWERE 14 May 1849.
     Funeral from residence, 2nd & Locust, Pittsburgh pc.

CAMPBELL, Mrs. Lucy, consort of Dr. Andrew, died in Platte   LEXA 16 May 1848
     Co. MO 25 Feb. Daughter of Rev. Edward Crawford
     of Washington Co. VA

CAMPBELL, Mrs. Sarah H., consort of David, died 9 Sept.   MORE 24 Oct 1844
     at Brunswick in her 53rd year. (David died a
     few weeks later, shown as " formerly of
     Knoxville, East Tenn.")

CANNON, Mary M. daughter of the late Col. Thomas died in   MORE 27 Mar 1849
     Nashville 22nd inst. Formerly of St. Louis.

CANOLE, Mrs. Jane, wife of Charles, died 20 May in her   BOLT 24 May 1845
     45th year. Baptist.

CANTER, Amanda P., daughter of the late Emanuel, died   MORE 13 Dec 1847
     "day before yesterday" age 18 years 6 mo.

CAPLES, Emily, consort of Rev. W. B., died at the home   BRUNS 27 Apr 1848
     of Wilson Elliott near Brunswick "Thursday last."
     Left 5 small children, one only a few weeks old.
     She was in her 29th year, daughter of General
     Gist "now of Weston."

CARLISLE, Mrs. Mary died yesterday morning. Funeral from   MORE 25 Aug 1841
     129 Market to Catholic Burying Ground.

CARMON, Nancy, wife of William, died 16 Feb. age   PWH 20 Feb 1841
     "about 40."

CARR, Emily, consort of Archibald, died Sunday 21 Feb.   MORE 25 Feb 1836
     in her 29th year, leaving husband and 2 infants.
     Interred Presbyterian cemetery.

CARR, Mrs. Anna Maria, wife of the Hon. William C.,   MORE 17 Aug 1826
     died 11 Aug. age 38.

CARROLL, Ann P., wife of Charles C., Esq. died in her   MORE 26 Jan 1846
     35th year. Funeral from residence, Chestnut St.
     between 7th & 8th.

CARRELL, Sarah, wife of John, died 17th inst. Late of   MORE 18 Sep 1848
     Louisville and formerly of Philadelphia.

CARTER, Mrs. Rebecca died Friday evening last, formerly   MORE 25 Jan 1839
     of Lowell, Mass.

CASE, Sally, consort of William died 29 Dec. in north   SWERE 10 Jan 1848
     St. Louis age 57. (Her husband died 7 January
     and is shown in the same issue with "Utica NY pc.")

CASS, Elizabeth, daughter of the Hon. Lewis, died at   MORE 14 Aug 1832
     Detroit in her 21st year.

CASSADY, Mrs. M. of Henry Co. died 19 June of diarrhoea   MORE 7 Oct 1850
     age 45.

CEARNALL, Mrs. Mary, wife of Archibald, died in her 58th year. Formerly of England. Baptist.   JEFRE 24 Aug 1839

CERRE, Therese, consort of Pascal, died 12 August.   MORE 13 Aug 1833

CHAMBERLAIN, Maria M., wife of Rev. Hiram, died 24 Mar. in Franklin. Daughter of Alpheus Morse of Essex, NY.   MIN 18 Apr 1835

CHAMBERLAIN, Mary Jane, eldest daughter of A. B. of Westfield, OH died 15 Jan. Had come to St. Louis "a few months since." Age 22.   SWERE 24 Jan 1848

CHAMBERLIN, Mrs. Ann, formerly of Jefferson Co. VA and eldest daughter of John Heller of St. Louis died Saturday last.   MORE 22 Oct 1839

CHAMBERLAIN, Sarah H., wife of Rev. H. of St. Charles died 18 May in Rockbridge, Conn., her birthplace, where she had gone for her health.   MORE 10 June 1840

CHANDLER, Rega consort of Henry died 10 Aug. age about 60.   PWH 12 Aug 1843

CHAPMAN, Hannah, widow of Rev. Robert H., died at the residence of her son, age 68.

CHENIE, Marie Therese, wife of Antoine Esq., died Saturday morning last age 56.   MORE 3 Feb 1840

CHENOWETH, Sarah Jane wife of Alfred died 26 Feb. age 30 y. 10m. 16 d.   SWERE 5 Mar 1849

CHEW, Sally, age 16, daughter of Mme. Manuel Lisa, died after a distressing illness of about 12 days.   MORE 22 Feb 1809

CHILD, Susan, wife of Thomas, died in Galena 24 Dec. Age 24, daughter of the late Henry Gratiot.   MORE 20 Jan 1844

CHILES, Emily D., wife of Col. F. P., died 20 March. Left husband, 2 stepchildren. Danville VA pc.   MORE 27 Mar 1846.

CHINN, Mary Ann, consort of R.T., died 11 Apr. in her 31st year. Left husband and 3 small children, the youngest only a few days old. Native of Spotsylvania Co., VA. Baptist.   WEM 25 Apr 1839

CHOUTEAU, Aurora, consort of P. L. and daughter of John Hay, died "yesterday morning."   MORE 11 Feb 1836

CHOUTEAU, Mrs. Brigitte, consort of Major Peter, Sr. died yesterday.   MORE 19 May 1829

CHOUTEAU, Mme. "the elder" (Therese) died "lately" leaving nearly 100 children, grandchildren, and great-grandchildren.   MORE 19 Nov 1814

CHRISTY, Martha, relict of William, died 26 April in her 72nd year. Funeral from Christ Church.   MORE 27 Apr 1849

CHRISTY, Miss Eliza P. S. died yesterday at the residence of J. D. Johnston. Age 18. Buried in the family graveyard at St. Charles.   MORE 11 July 1839

CHRISTY, Mrs. "wife of Wm. Christy Esq." died "last Saturday" MORE 23 July 1823

CLACK, Mrs. "wife of Rev. Spencer" died of cholera in Palmyra. MORE 28 June 1833

CLAFLIN, Nancy W., wife of William, died Saturday. formerly of Milton, Mass. MORE 10 Jan 1842

CLAIRMONT, Mrs. Marianne died 25 Feb. at Portage des Sioux, age 76. MORE 3 March 1845

CLARK, Mrs. Ann Bronson died in Independence 19 May age 35. Formerly of Boston. MORE 27 May 1849

CLARK, Mrs. Martha, wife of Bennet Esq., died 25 June. MIN 2 July 1822

CLARK, Eleanor Atkinson, wife of Henry L., died 23 June in her 25th year. Funeral residence, 92 Elm St. MORE 24 June 1844

CLARK, Eleanor, wife of L. B., died age 52. MORE 24 June 1849

CLARK, Elizabeth, wife of Thomas, formerly of St. Louis Co., was murdered in Warren Co. by a negress she had threatened to punish. Age 55. MORE 11 May 1846

CLARK, Harriet, wife of Gen. William, died 25 Dec. MORE 27 Dec 1831

CLARK, Jane Elizabeth of Monticello, Mo. died Monday last, only daughter of Hon. James A. and Martha A. decd. Age 14 y 11 m 8 d. BRUNS 30 Dec 1848

CLARKE, Mary Warren, wife of Robert, died 25 April. Residence #143 6th St. MORE 26 Apr 1849

CLARK, Mrs. Judith died at the residence of Capt. C. Anderson in her 30th year. Born in Campbell Co. VA. Left aged mother Mrs. Moorman. Widow of Henry Clark. Methodist. (Callaway Co.) MORE 12 Apr 1842

CLARKSON, Marion, wife of Dr. H. M., formerly of Fauquier Co. VA died 5 Dec. COP 9 Dec 1842

CLAY, Amira wife of George died at Little Rock 8 Dec. age 48. Lexington KY pc. MORE 24 Sep 1846

CLAY, Mary Ann Gamalia, wife of Cyprian, a printer, died age 23 years. Funeral from house of Samuel Bosworth, 9 Olive St. MORE 19 Sep 1838

CLEMENT, Martha Ann, consort of Abraham, died 13 May. Of Cole Co., MO. Formerly of Pittsylvania Co. VA. Left husband, 5 children. MORE 22 May 1840

CLENDENNEN, Mrs., wife of William, died 19 Jan. age 66. Married 47 years, raised 10 children, 9 of whom were living in Cole Co. JEFRE 10 Feb 1844.

CLOYD, Mahala, consort of D.P., died 5 Oct. MODE 14/10 Oct 1846

COATES, Mrs. Francis, consort of T.P. of Randolph Co. died 7 March in her 43rd year, 4 little children. Louisville pc. (BOLT 16 Apr gives initials F. P.) MORE 18 Mar 1842

COCHRAN, Mary Ann, daughter of James of Carrollton,   BRUNS 7 Apr 1849
   died aboard the steamboat Falcon returning
   after 2 years in Virginia. Buried beside her
   mother in the Thomas graveyard.

COFFEE, Mrs. Catherine G., wife of Col. John T. of   SPAD 22 Oct 1844
   Greenfield, Dade Co., died at the residence of
   Capt. John Hunt in Polk Co. in her 17th year.
   Left an infant daughter.

COHEN, Amanda Melvina, oldest daughter of Thomas, died   MORE 22 Jan 1833
   in her 16th year.
   Mary Louisa, daughter of Thomas, died 10 June.   MORE 18 June 1833

COLBURN, Martha L., wife of Norris Esq., died 8 March   MORE 9 Mar 1841
   in her 29th year, of consumption. Formerly
   of Fitzwilliam, New Hampshire.

COLE, Mme. Therese Bosseron, wife of Samuel, died   MORE 9 July 1841
   8 Aug. Interred Catholic cemetery.

COLLET, Ann died Monday evening last in her 84th   MORE 23 Dec 1840
   year. Interred Episcopal cemetery.

COLLIER, Catherine died in St. Charles 5 June age 74.   MORE 9 June 1835
   Had lived in St. Charles 17 years, had been
   a widow 35 years.

COLLIER, Euphrasie F., wife of Mr. Collier, died Sunday.   SCOMB 2 Sep 1835
   (This same issue reports the death of Louisa,
   eldest child of George, Esq., but whether they
   were mother and child is not clear.)

COLLINS, Mrs. Barbara died 24 August.   MORE 1 Sep 1829

COLVIN, Rosanna wife of John died in Calumet Twp.   BGRAD 9 Nov 1844
   20 October.

COMMONS, Mary widow of the late Thomas died 30 Nov.   SWERE 3 Dec 1848
   age 52.

COMSTOCK, Elizabeth C., wife of James F., died 8 Feb.   MORE 9 Feb 1842
   Funeral from the residence of Aaron
   Comstock, Washington between 4th & 5th.

CONN, Mrs. Isabella, died yesterday at the residence   MORE 9 Feb 1844
   of her son-in-law Wayman Crow.

CONNOLLY, Catherine, wife of Peter, died in her 34th   MORE 26 Dec 1848
   year.

CONSAUD   Rachel, wife of Col. Joseph of St. Louis,   MORE 9 Feb 1844
(CONSAUL?) daughter of Abraham de Groff Esq. of
   Schenectady, died 7 Feb. Was in St. Louis
   only a year and a few months.

CONSE, Leontine, wife of James M., died 12 April.   MORE 13 Apr 1836
   Residence, 2nd St. between Olive & Pine.

CONWAY, Mrs. S., consort of F. R., died Friday.   MORE 15 July 1834
   Mrs. Martha, consort of F.R., age 39, at   BRUNS 14 June 1849
   (MORE 2 June: ae 39 y 3 d)   St. Louis

COOK, Lydia Ann, consort of Langford, died Sunday in her 30th year.   MODE 28 Mar 1848

COOK, Mrs. Sophronia, died yesterday at the residence of her brother Col. Wm. L. Sublette.   MORE 21 Apr 1843

COOLEY, Ellen died at the residence of her brother-in-law L. G. Conklin on Green St.   MORE 17 May 1849

COOPER, Mrs. Ann Eliza, consort of D.F., died 28 Sept.   BOLT 1 Oct 1842

COOPER, Priscilla, consort of Jacob, died Wednesday last.   MORE 24 Dec 1835

COOPER, Mrs. Sarah E. A. W. died 13th inst in her 28th year.   PWH 15 May 1841

CORBIN, Mary Egerton, wife of A.D., rector of Christ Church, Boonville, died at the residence of her father Daniel Hough.   MORE 30 Apr 1846

CORCORAN, Miss Nancy died in her 25th year.   MORE 26 June 1849

COREN, Catherine died Wednesday age 60. Cincinnati pc.   MORE 25 Dec 1843

CORMACK, Cecelia, wife of John B., died 8 Sept.   SWERE 16 Sep 1844

CORNELIUS, Frances consort of Abner died "in this county" 18 March.   MIN 2 Apr 1830

COULTER, Mrs. died Monday last at the residence of Edward Bates Esq.   MORE 4 July 1825

COURSAULT, Mrs. E. died 20 Oct. after a 2-day illness. Native of France, she was for many years a resident of Baltimore and St. Louis.   MORE 7 Nov 1834

COUZINS, Mrs. P. J., wife of James W., died 15 Sept. (Also her infant.) Residence #7 2nd St., opposite Green Tree. New York pc. Buried Episcopal graveyard.   MORE 16 Sep 1841.

COWPERTHWAIT, Eliza, wife of William P. of St. Louis, died in New York 17th inst ae 26.   MORE 27 Sep 1847

COXE, Mrs. Lucy Ann, consort of Henry, Esq. died yesterday.   MORE 9 July 1833

CRAWFORD, Mrs. Ellen wife of James E. died age 28. Presbyterian. Staunton *Spectator* pc.   PWH 5 March 1846

CRAWLEY, Mrs. Elizabeth wife of Maj. Jonathan died 19 September.   MIN 20 Sep 1827

CRISSWELL, Mrs. ___ wife of H. died 25th inst.   INP 4 Mar 1826

CROCKER, Jennetta, consort of Hiram, died 22 May. Baptist Church, Lebanon.   JINQ 30 June 1842

CROMWELL, Mrs. Ann Elizabeth died Sunday.   BEA 30 Aug 1832

CROWE, Aramintha, consort of Benoni S., died 9 Jan. in Jefferson Co. Native of Pennsylvania.   MORE 22 Jan 1848

CRUESS, Mary, wife of Peter, died 21st inst. Interred in Episcopal burying ground.   MORE 23 Feb 1842

CRUSON, Mrs., consort of K., died last evening.	MORE 3 May 1833
CRUTCHFIELD, Mrs. Elizabeth of Lewis Co. died 30 Oct. age 65.	PWH 6 Nov 1835
CULVER, Pamela A., wife of Henry, formerly of Maryland, died 1 March.	MORE 2 Mar 1838
CUMMINS, Mrs. James, accidentally shot by husband in Atchison Co. "a few days since."	BRUNS 20 Jan 1849
CUMMINS, Mrs. Eliza died 26 Sept. at the house of Mr. John C. Gray near the Chalk Banks of the Mississippi, after a long and painful illness, in her 26th year. Consort of A.M., late of New Orleans, Natchez, Tennessee, and Alabama. Leaves husband, "three helpless children."	MORE 10 Oct 1821
CUNNINGHAM, Mrs. Hannah, age about 45, died Thursday last in Buffalo Twp, Pike Co.	BGDB 17 May 1845
CUNNINGHAM, Mrs. Martha, consort of N. C. of St. Louis died at the residence of her father, Wm. Scott, Howard Co., 18 June.	MODE 1 July 1846
CUNNINGHAM, Mary, wife of Arthur and sister of Thomas and Francis Nugent died 10 May age 25.	SWERE 14 May 1849
CUNNINGHAM, Susan, wife of James of Boone Co., died 4 Sept. age 59.	MIN 19 Sep 1835
DADE, Mrs. A., consort of John, died in Boonville on 23 July. Left 4 young children.	MORE 4 Sep 1832
DAGGETT, Eliza, died 19th inst age 50. Residence Olive St. between 9th & 10th.	MORE 20 Nov 1846
DALY, Mrs. Elizabeth, relict of Lawrence J., died 13 October. Left numerous relatives both in MO and KY. Age about 71. Many years member of the United Baptist Church.	MODE 13/11 Oct 1847 COMB 22 Oct 1847
DALLAM, Frances D., wife of Josias M., Esq. died 14th inst in 54th year. Formerly of Hartford Co. MD.	MORE 17 July 1841
DALLAM, Mrs. Priscilla, wife of R.B. Esq., died 23rd inst in her 61st year. Methodist. Left children. Miss Louisa, 3rd daughter of R. B., died on Tuesday last in 18th year. Recently of Kentucky, formerly of Hartford Co. MD	MORE 25 Feb 1840 MORE 11 Jan 1831
DANGEN, Miss Celina, daughter of the late Antoine, died Friday last.	MORE 1 June 1830
Mrs. Clara Marguerette, relict of the late Antoine, died last Sunday.	MORE 12 July 1842
DANGEN, Mrs.__, consort of John P., died "a few days DONGEN since" in St. Louis Co., age 50.	SLINQ 18 Aug 1821
DANIELS, Miss Virginia died in the Jackson vicinity 4th inst. age 50(?).	INP 3/10 Aug 1822

DARGEN, Mrs. Margaret died at the residence of her son-in-law J. S. Findley near Lexington, Lafayette Co., on 21 June. Native of Maryland. Many years resident of Washington DC. Methodist 40 years. MIN 13 July 1826

DAVIDSON, Camilla died of consumption in Franklin Co. 24 May. MOAR 12 June 1835

DAVISSON, Mrs. Cassandra, relict of the late Daniel of Bonhomme, died 7 September. MORE 17 Sep 1823

DAVIDSON, Dialtha, consort of John P., died 31 Sept. in Brunswick. BRUNS 12 Aug 1848

DAVIS, Therese Katherine Vasquez, wife of D. D. Esq., died in her 28th year. Catholic cemetery. New York and Detroit pc. MORE 16 Apr 1846

DAVIS, Eliza, wife of Alfred P., died 30 Dec. COMB 31 Dec 1846

DAVIS, Eliza, consort of George, died yesterday, in St. Louis. MORE 2 Apr 1836

DAVIS, Elizabeth Jane, consort of Horatio N., died 12th inst in her 27th year. Pittsburgh, Philadelphia, and Baltimore pc. MORE 15 July 1845

DAVIS, Margaret Annis, youngest daughter of Col. Wm. C., died at Marshall, Saline Co., in her 22nd year, on 21 March. Formerly of Augusta Co. VA BOLT 5 Apr 1845

DAVIS, Rebecca Franc_is_, daughter of Rev. Samuel C., died 19th inst in Randolph Co. in her 17th y. BOLT 26 Oct 1844

DAVIS, Rebecca J., a highly respectable teacher, committed suicide by hanging 14 June. Ae 35-40. MORE 22 June 1844

DAVIS, Sarah Ann, consort of Rev. Jesse P., died at Fredericktown 16th inst ae 24. Left infant son. MORE 24 Sep 1844

DAVIS, Mrs. Sarah Elizabeta, wife of James Hunter and daughter of John J. Lowry of Howard Co., died in her 21st year in Randolph Co. 27 Sept. Left husband and infant child. BOLT 12 Oct 1844

DAVIS, Susan F., wife of Simon, died age 37. Left large family of children. STGAZ 22 Nov 1845

DAWSON, Mary E. died in St. Joseph 14 Nov. STGAZ 19 Nov 1847

DAY, Mrs. Catherine, died near Mexico in Audrain Co., consort of Lewis, in her 52nd year. Methodist. FULT 15 Sep 1848

DAY, Cynthia Ann Stonebraker, wife of Capt. Henry R., daughter of John, sister-in-law of John Orrick, died 8 Feb. age 22. Episcopal cemetery. MORE 9 Feb 1847,

DeBANN, Sarah Ann, wife of George, died 5th inst ae 29. Residence 185 Locust. MORE 6 Mar 1849

DeBAR, Mary, consort of Benjamin, late of St. Louis and New Orleans theatres, died aboard the steamboat _Eliza_ from New Orleans Sunday last. MORE 4 Nov 1841

DeBONNEVILLE, Mme. Margaret, native of France, died at an advanced age.	MORE 31 Oct 1846
DeCAMP, Mary Augusta, consort of Lt. John, died 26th inst at Jefferson Barracks, age 26.	MORE 29 July 1843
DEEDS, Melissa P. died Saturday morning.	SPAD 11 Oct 1845
DEFORD, Mrs. Susan, consort of Rev. Joseph M., died at Warsaw "the 23rd" age 43.	JEM 21 Dec 1847
DeHODIAMONT, Mrs. Caroline widow of Emanuel died at River des Peres 29th inst.	MORE 31 Jan 1832
DeLISLE, Catherine, relict of Louis, died 8 July in St. Louis age 77.	MORE 9 July 1840
DEMENT, Mary Catherine consort of William died 14 Dec.	CAMP 15 Dec 1848
DEMEREE, Mrs. Eliza died Monday age 23, leaving husband and child.	BEA 22 Apr 1830
DEMETTE, Emilie, consort of Francois, died 13th inst age 65. Residence 126 S. 3rd St.	MORE 14 Aug 1848
DEMETTE, Mary Louise died 30 Oct. in her 23rd year.	MORE 2 Nov 1846
DEMIE, Mrs. Josephine died at the residence of Mrs. A. Valle (5th & Elm). She was 76, a native of Santo Domingo.	MORE 27 Aug 1842
DERRICKSON, Emily, wife of Charles, formerly of St. Louis, died of cholera. Left 2 children.	BRUNS 5 July 1849
DETCHEMENDY, Alitia Camilla Wathen, wife of Clement C., died in Ste. Genevieve 27 Aug. "His children mourn her as a second mother"	MOAR 27 Sep 1838 SMAD 8 Sep 1838
DEVER, Mrs. Ann, relict of Henry, died near St. Louis 8th inst age 47.	MORE 9 Jan 1835
DEAVER, Sophia Augusta died Friday 21st inst age 17.	MORE 22 June 1839
DEVOE, Mrs. Sarah Ann, consort of William, died 18th inst.	MORE 30 Oct 1832
DICKERSON, Eliza and infant, formerly of Portsmouth OH died in the hospital. She was 25.	MORE 20 June 1840
DIGGS, Catherine C., consort of Francis W., died at at Glasgow 16 Dec. age 40.	BRUNS 30 Dec 1848
DIGGES, Miss Georgiana, daughter of Whitting and Sarah, died 2 Oct. age 27.	BRUNS 7 Oct 1848
DIGGES, Miss Elizabeth died at Glasgow 17 July in her 19th year.	BOLT 27 July 1844
DILLINGER, Mrs. Catherine, age 63, died 4 June. She was a native of Washington Co. MD, resided on Moreau Creek; had apoplexy 23 May, became paralyzed 30 May. Left children.	JINQ 8 June 1843
DISHAROON, Mrs. Hetty, wife of T., died 13th inst near St. Louis in 34th year. Native of Snow Hill Worcester Co. MD	22 Feb 1840 MORE

DISHROON, Miss Amelia died in St. Louis 1 July.   MORE 2 July 1835
    Helen Mary died 13 July. Interred   MORE 14 July 1835
    Methodist burying ground.

DOCKER, Elizabeth Smith, wife of Dr. William, died   MORE 26 Nov 1844
    at Commerce, Scott Co., 3 Nov. in her 37th
    year. They were English, immigrating, lost all
    their property in a steamboat wreck in August
    1840 and had remained where they were.

DODD, Miss Margaret, age 69, died at the residence of   MIN 25 Sep 1821
    Col. George Knox in Franklin.

DODGE, Mrs. Catherine died 16 January in her 72nd yr.   MOAR 19 Feb 1836

DODGE, Elizabeth W, wife of Ezra, died 21 May.   MORE 24 May 1845

DOLMAN, Sarah C., wife of John H. died 11 June.   BRUNS 21 June 1849

DONNER, Miss Sarah, niece of J. Horine, died near   MORE 5 Apr 1820
    Herculaneum 15 March.

DOREY, Grace, wife of John, died 6 Sept. age 65.   SLDU 2 Sep 1846

DORR, Mrs. Frances, wife of Lieut. Joseph, died at   MORE 2 Nov. 1808
    Camp Bellefontaine after a short illness.

DORRIS, Jane, daughter of Dr. S. C., died 17 May   JEFRE 23 May 1835
    age 16.

DORSEY, Catherine S., consort of George, died at   WEM 6 Feb 1840
    Boonville age 27. Left one child.

DOUGHERTY, Lucy J. H., consort of William D., died   MORE 29 May 1847
    21 May in her 25th year.

DOW, Mrs. C., wife of James, died in Fayette last   MIN 23 Oct 1829
    Friday.

DOWNEY, Mrs., died the 22nd, an aged lady of this   BOLT 29 Aug 1840
    county.

DOWNEY, Anne, wife of William, died 3 Sept. age   MODE 30/28 Sep 1846
    47 y 9 d. Baptist about 27 years.

DOXEY, Rebecca, wife of John, died 19 May age about   BOLT 26 May 1846
    55; of Bowling Green Prairie, Chariton Co.

DOYLE, Hannah, wife of Dr. J. D., of High Point,   MORE 11 Sep 1847
    Moniteau Co., died 25 Aug. in her 56th year.
    Left 5 children. Trenton NJ and Madison IA pc.

DOYLE, Sister Melania, died 23rd June at the Hospital.   MORE 24 June 1846
    Native of West Meath.

DOYLE, Sarah Frances, died at the residence of A. H.   MORE 21 Oct 1841
    Evans, #2 7th St. Interred City burying ground.

DRAKE, Martha Ellen Taylor, wife of Charles D., Esq.,   MORE 17 Jan 1842
    died in her 30th year. Funeral from residence,
    5th St. between Olive & Locust. Presbyterian
    burying ground.

DRAPER, Mrs. Sarah M. died in North St. Louis   MORE 10 July 1844
    5 July in her 26th year.

DUBREUIL, Emilie died 21 Dec. age 25. Funeral from residence of her brother Louis, #124 N. 3d. Catholic burying ground.	MORE 22 Dec 1847
DUCHOQUETTE, Mrs. Zelie, consort of John B., died Wednesday, 3 July.	MORE 5 July 1833
DUDLEY, Mary Thornton daughter of Col. P. died 28th inst.	PWH 31 Dec 1842
DUFOUR, Eveline, comsort of Pierre, daughter of Jedediah Allen and sister of the late Beverly Allen, died in Ste. Genevieve 8 Jan. age 34.	MORE 21 Jan 1846
DUGGETT, Lucy Ann died Friday last, daughter of John Duggett.	MORE 12 Feb 1833
DUNBAR, Mrs. Elizabeth, consort of Thomas, died 29 August in her 31st year. Baptist.	BGRAD 2 Sep 1843
DUNCAN, Mrs. Caroline, consort of Thomas O., died 22nd inst in her 28th year leaving husband and 3 small children.	MORE 26 Oct 1830
DUNLAP, Jane died 12th inst age 57. Residence 5th St.	MORE 14 May 1849
DUNN, Mrs. Martha of St. Louis died 13 June near Ash Hollow (on the trail west) age 19.	MORE 7 Oct 1850
DUNN, Mary Jane, daughter of James, Esq. of near Warsaw, Benton Co., died 10 Aug. in her 27th year.	MODE 25/23 Aug 1847
DUNNICA, Maria E., consort of Capt. Theodore W., died 10 July at the home of her brother-in-law, J. H. Schweppe, in Alton. Daughter of decd. J. Poiner, Esq., late of Lynchburgh VA. Methodist. Funeral from Planter's House.	MORE 12 July 1847
DUNNICA, Mrs. Philadelphia P., consort of James, died 31 May (her infant died the day previous). In the 43rd year of her age; left several children.	MORE 19 June 1832
DUNNINGTON, Mrs. Ann, died 16 June in her 73rd year. Formerly of Glasgow; came to Brunswick with son-in-law Dr. Bull. Methodist.	BRUNS 24 June 1848
DuPRESLIN, Mrs. A. died 3 Jan. in her 72nd year. Formerly of Charleston SC.	MORE 4 Jan 1847
DURKEE, Julia, wife of Dwight Rsq. died 30 March aboard the steamboat _Anthony_. Age 30. Funeral from Christ Church.	SWERE 2 Apr 1849
DUSENBURY, Gertrude, wife of Dr. R. T., died Monday. Daughter of D. Van Epps, Fulton, Oswego Co. New York. Residence Franklin-9th-10th Sts.	MORE 28 Feb 1843
DWYER, Ann, consort of Jeremiah, died yesterday age 33.	SWERE 24 Apr 1848
DYE, Mrs. Arminty wife of John died 20th inst leaving a large family.	PWH 28 Jan 1847

EARLL, Mrs. Sybil Emeline died in St. Louis 16 Oct.	MORE 23 Oct 1832
EARNEST, Pamelia Ann daughter of Robert L. died in Carroll Co. age 18. Methodist. Nashville Christian Advocate pc.	BRUNS 16 Aug 1849
EASTON, Abial wife of Rufus died in St. Charles 22 Feb.	MORE 23 Feb 1849
EATON, Mrs. James died in Shelby Co. 2 Sept.	PWH 16 Sep 1843
ECHOLS, Mrs. Eliza wife of J. W. of Scott Co. died aboard a steamboat at Randolph while on her to Washata Springs.	SMAD 27 Apr 1838
EDDY, Phoebe died at the residence of her son-in-law J. Glenny 13 Dec. in her 75th year. Native of Lebanon Co., Ohio. Lebanon pc.	MORE 17 Dec 1844
EDELIN, Miss Ann, daughter of Aloysius Esq., died in Louisville, Lincoln Co. MO "Wednesday last."	SALT 15 May 1841
EDGAR, Sarah A. T., wife of Rev. S. L., died 3 Feb. in Ray Co. of consumption. Daughter of Robert Baker of Logan Co. KY. Left "offspring."	LEXP 11 Mar 1845
EDMUNDSON, Mrs. Francis H., Esq. died 16 June.	PWH 19 June 1841
EDMUNDSTON, Lucretia wife of Eden died 23 Nov in her 52nd year. Mary Elizabeth daughter of Eden died 14 Nov. in her 13th year.	MORE 4 Feb 1843
EDWARDS, Irena Z., consort of William B., died in Dallas Co. 17th inst.	SPAD 26 Sep 1846
EDWARDS, Miss Julia died recently in the vicinity of Jefferson City. Sister of Gov. Edwards.	MORE 19 Feb 1845
EDWARDS, Elvira Lane, relict of Ninian, late governor of Illinois, died in St. Louis 5 June at the residence of John P. Cabanne.	MORE 7 June 1839
EDWARDS, Mrs. Sarah, mother of Gov. Edwards, died in Springfield MO 6 Dec.	MODE 6 Dec 1847
EIKEN, Mrs. Elizabeth died age 19.	JINQ 19 Sep 1844
ELGIN, Mary Frances daughter of William H. & Clemency died 16 Aug. in her 11th year.	BOLT 16 Aug 1845
ELLET, Laura, wife of John J. of St. Louis, died at Monticello IL 4 Aug. age 34.	SWERE 9 Aug 1847
ELLIOTT, Mrs. Ethelinda, wife of Dr. William, died at Goshen NY 14 Aug. age 65.	MORE 22 Sep 1829
ELLIOTT, Ann, relict of Dr. Aaron of Ste. Genevieve, died 1 Sept.	MORE 19 Sep 1811
ELLIOTT, Maria wife of Capt. Edward and late a resident died in New Orleans 18 Aug. in her 57th year. Eliza their daughter died in New Orleans 20 Aug. age 30.	MORE 30 Aug 1847
ELLIS, Elizabeth wife of Dr. R. B., senator from Daviess Co. died 2 March.	JINQ 9 Mar 1843

ELLIS, Mrs. Polly, died in St. Louis yesterday, age about 65. Widow of Dr. Erasmus of Cape Girardeau. — MORE 16 July 1844

ELY, Mary Ann, wife of Rev. Ezra Stiles Ely and daughter of S. Carswell, decd. of Philadelphia died at West Ely 14 Sept. in her 50th year. — PWH 17 Sep 1842

EMERSON, Mary Ann, consort of Eaton, died in Brunswick 11 Jan. Left 4 children. — BRUNS 26 Jan 1848

EMMONS, Mrs. Elizabeth died 17 Aug. in St. Charles, age 80. Formerly of Woodstock, Vermont. — MORE 29 Aug 1825

ENGLISH, Mrs. Martha Augusta, wife of James Lawrence English and daughter of Edward Worthington, formerly of Mercer Co. KY, died suddenly at Georgetown MO 19th inst in her 23rd year. — MORE 1 Feb 1838

ENGLISH, Mrs. Elizabeth, late of St. Louis, consort of Capt. Samuel, died at Beaver PA 19 June. — MORE 17 July 1832

ESCHENBURG, Isabel daughter of John, Esq. died yesterday age 12. Episcopal cemetery. — MORE 4 Feb 1846

ESSEX, Mrs. Cecelia A., wife of W. T., died 16 April age 21y 1m 1d. — MORE 18 Apr 1849

EUBANK, Mrs. and 2 children died of cholera in Palmyra. — MORE 28 June 1833

EUSTACE, Mrs., wife of Rev., died as a result of burns received when a lamp exploded. (Her husband, Thomas, was a Presbyterian minister.) — MORE 29 Oct 1845

EVANS, Mrs. Mildred, consort of Augustus H., died yesterday. — MORE 2 Feb 1830
Mary Ann, wife of A. H., died 27 Aug. age 28 on Laclede Ave. two miles from St. Louis. — MORE 6 Sep 1847

EVANS, Anna Maria wife of Prof. Evans died 19th inst age 42. Was injured in a stagecoach wreck and survived about two weeks. — MORE 30 Sep 1846

EVANS, Eliza, wife of D. Esq. and daughter of Capt. E. (Elliott? see Maria Elliott) died in New Orleans 20 August age 30. — MORE 2 Sep 1847

EWIN, Miss Euphemia, only daughter of Watts D., died 20 August in her 20th year. — BOLT 23 Aug 1845

EWING, Harriet, wife of Col. T. W., died 24th inst in her 37th year. Formerly of Peru, IN. Resided at 5th & Carr. Catholic cemetery. — MORE 26 Jan 1847

EWING, Mrs. Polly, widow of Maj. Urbin, died 18 Sept. in Lafayette Co. Mother of W. Y. C. Ewing, commissioner of school lands. — MIN 29 Sep 1832

FALLON, Susan, consort of William of St. Louis Co., died 29 Dec. age 34. — MORE 5 Jan 1844

FANNING, Susan, wife of Samuel, died 31 Dec. Resided on Olive St. between 15th & 16th. — MORE 1 Jan 1849

FANT, Mrs. Charles died Sunday last.	MOP 23 Aug 1846
FARISH, Rebecca died at the home of her brother-in-law Rev. F. E. McElroy in Hannibal in her 38th year. Native of Virginia, widowed young, she lived with her mother Mrs. Porter in Troy.	MORE 6 Apr 1848
FARMER, Nancy G., wife of W. W. Esq. of Dade Co., died 29th inst. Daughter of John Sommerville, formerly of Clarksburg VA.	PWH 27 Sep 1849
FARNHAM, Susan, relict of Russell, died Saturday.	23 July 1833 MORE
FARNSWORTH, Abigail died at Dardenne, St. Charles Co., 4 Sept. Wife of Alden.	MORE 27 Sep 1827
FARR, Sarah, consort of Col. Woodson, died near Glasgow. Age 21.	BRUNS 14 Oct 1848
FARRAR, Mrs. Frances died at the home of Andrew Martin in her 67th year, of pulmonary consumption. Daughter of Mr. Brown, born in Virginia, raised in North Carolina. Mother of 7 children, of whom 4 predeceased her. Baptist since age 22.	INP 13 May 1826
FARRAR, Mrs. Sarah S., consort of Dr. B. G., died of consumption "Monday last."	MORE 8 Nov 1817
FARRELL, Mrs. Mary, wife of John W., died 22nd inst. Residence Morgan near 6th. Left husband and 2 sons; one son predeceased her.	MORE 23 Apr 1841
FARRIS, Catherine Ann, consort of Robert P., Esq. died Wednesday night last.	MORE 17 Mar 1829
FASSEU, Mrs. Phillippine, consort of Louis E., native of Neufchatel, Switz. died 20th inst at her residence in Carondelet, in her 51st year.	MORE 28 Nov 1836
FEAGEN, Mrs. Sarah died at a very advanced age on Thursday last.	PWH 29 Jan 1845
FERGUSON, Eliza Susan died at the residence of John McCausland, age about 16 (?). (She had an estate in the St. Louis Probate records.) Episcopal burying ground.	MORE 17 July 1841
FERGUSON, Mary Susan died yesterday at the residence of her father John H. Gay, 4th & Myrtle.	MORE 11 July 1846
FIELDS, Elizabeth of Harrison Co. died at Chimney Rock 16 June, age 17, of cholera.	MORE 7 Oct 1850
FINCH, Eliza Ann, wife of William F., died yesterday age 32. Left children. Resided Franklin & 7th.	MORE 19 Dec 1843
FINCH, Permelia Ann, wife of William T., died age 28y 3m. Resided 7th St. Cincinnati and Milwaukee pc.	MORE 20 June 1849
FISHER, Sarah, wife of E., died 9 Feb. age 38y 5m 26 d. Native of Delaware. Mother & wife.	JINQ 10 Feb 1842 JEFRE 12 Feb "
FITHIAN, Mrs. Capt. and infant daughter died 12th inst at residence of her brother John H. Bernard.	MORE 13 Aug 1842

FITZHUGH, Mrs. Fanny died 19 June at the residence of   MORE 20 June 1825
   Col. John O'Fallon. Late of Louisville KY.

FITZ-RANDOLPH, Julia, daughter of Robert of New York   MORE 5 Nov 1823
   and only sister of Mrs. Post of Bonhomme
   died 1 Oct. at the house of Wickliffe G.
   Post near Mt. Pleasant, Green Co. IL

FLANDRY, Mrs. Margaret, native of Vincennes, died Sunday   MORE 8 Feb 1838
   evening, 4 Feb., in Carondelet. A resident of
   St. Louis Co. for 70 years.

FLEMING, Mrs. P. E., wife of Dr. N. L., died at the   MORE 25 Jan 1847
   home of her father S. P. Harris in St. Francois
   Co. 9 June. Left 3 small children.

FLOOD, Mary Ellen, wife of Juge J. J. and daughter of   MODE 21/19 Oct 1846
   D. Prewitt, Es. died at Linnaues 3rd inst.
   Formerly of Howard Co.

FOLEY, Mrs. Ann age 36 died at the home of her brother   SLDU 9 Oct 1846
   Nicholas Tiernan 8th inst. Funeral from St. Fcis
   Xavier Church to Catholic cemetery.

FOOT, Mrs. Ann Treadwell, wife of Dr., died 6th inst at   MORE 30 Oct 1832
   Fort Crawford.

FORBES, Harriet W., wife of Leonard, died in New York   SWERE 4 Oct 1847
   5 Sept. Funeral from residence of George   MORE 2 Oct 1847
   Frothingham to Presbyterian cemetery.

FORD, Agnes Ann died at Waterloo, Clark Co. MO on   MORE 3 Sep 1841
   Sunday 22 Aug. in her 23rd year. Consort of
   Thomas D.

FOREE, Margaret E., daughter of William P. and Eliza J.   MORE 17 Feb 1844
   died near Christiansburg KY 7th inst in her
   18th year.

FOREY, Mrs. Rachel, consort of Dr. F. Dory (?) late of   MORE 4 Jan 1845
   of Louisville died 3rd inst. Funeral from her
   residence, Broadway 3 doors from the Mound.
   Interred Illinois.

FORSYTH, Mrs. S., consort of Major Thomas, died at her   MORE 1 Dec 1829
   residence near St. Louis Saturday 21 Nov.

FOSTER, Ann Ives, oldest daughter of Eli, died 21st   SLDU 23 Oct 1846
   inst in her 22nd year.

FOSTER, Mildred wife of the late John died 11 Sept.   PWH 17 Sep 1845
   age about 25.

FOSTER, Mary C., relict of John L. of Pittsylvania Co.   MORE 1 May 1849
   VA died 26th ult.

FOSTER, Sarah wife of John J. died 10th inst in her 30th   MORE 23 Oct 1841
   year in Callaway Co. MO. Formerly of Prince
   Edward Co. VA.

FOSTER, Mrs. Sarah, consort of Joseph, died yesterday   MORE 25 Mar 1845
   age 37.

FRANCISCUS, Eliza Jane, eldest daughter of John Esq., formerly of Baltimore, died 1 Aug. at Lewistown PA.	MORE 7 July 1847
FRAZIER, Drewsyla, wife of Robert, died 25 Dec. in Creve Coeur. Left a small family.	SLINQ 13 Jan 1821
FRAZER, Martha, wife of John S. and daughter of Mrs. (Elizabeth) O'Conner died age 30. Left one son.	PWH 26 Mar 1842
FRAZIER, Mary A., wife of John, died 12th inst age 25 in Hillsboro, Jefferson Co. (Her daughter Anna, age 3y 11 d, died on the 18th).	BRUNS 2 Aug 1849
FREELAND, Miss Amanda, daughter of Col. William F., died 12 July, ten miles from St. Louis.	MORE 18 July 1825
FREELAND, Mrs. Elizabeth, wife of Robert, died at the residence of Wm. Talbot, Loutre Island, on 27 Feb. in her 25th year. Left husband and one child. (She was the daughter of Warner Lewis; her sister Jane married Wm. Talbot.)	MORE 13 Mar 1839
FROST, Mary, wife of Samuel, died at Steelville, Crawford Co., age 49y 8m.	JEFRE 14 Dec 1839
FULKERSON, Mary M., consort of Isaac of St. Charles Co. died 12th inst of consumption in her 26th year. Left one little daughter. Cape Girardeau and Jackson, MO pc.	MORE 26 Apr 1836
FULKERSON, Sarah, relict of Frederick, died in Lafayette Co. 29 March.	LEXP 8 Apr 1845
GAAR, Mrs. Almira E. M., consort of M. F. Esq., died near Franklin 3rd inst age 34. Married 16 years. (Her son James age 3 died at the same time, both of measles.)	MODE 29/27 Apr 1846
GAINES, Mrs. Sydney Ann died Thursday in her 38th year.	BOLT 11 May 1844
GANNAWAY, Sarah wife of John B. died 7 March near Roanoke (MO) in her 28th year.	MODE 14 Mar 1848
GANTT, Mrs. Ann, consort of the Rev. Edward of Louisville, died 17th ult after a short illness.	MORE 26 May 1819
GANTT, Mrs. Virginia, wife of the late Capt., US Army, died Wednesday morning last.	MORE 22 Nov 1833
GARDNER, Ellen wife of Thomas died in St. Ferdinand Twp. 13th inst. age 22.	MORE 23 Jan 1849
GARLAND, Mrs. Hannah wife of Dr. Isaac died at the Des Moines Rapids, Mississippi River.	MORE 17 Apr 1832
GARNER, Mrs. Catherine died at the residence of her son William 7th inst age 87.	PWH 13 Nov 1845
GARNETT, Mrs. R. of Jefferson City. (No date)	JINQ 5 Oct 1843
GARRATY, Mrs., consort of Joseph, died yesterday.	MORE 6 Dec 1831

GARNETT, Elizabeth, consort of William of Round Grove   PWH 27 Feb 1841
    Twp., died 17 Feb. leaving 5 children. Baptist.

GARRETT, Mrs., wife of Reuben, one of the oldest citizens   JEFRE 7 Oct 1843
    of Cole Co., died Wednesday last.

GARRISON, Margaret Jane, consort of Daniel R., died 7th   MORE 11 Jan 1840
    inst in her 21st year. Formerly of Pittsburgh.
    Left a 3-wk-old baby.

GARTRELL, Mrs. "an old lady" died of cholera in Palmyra.   JEFRE 4 July 1835

GAY, Adaline B., wife of John L. Esq. of Livingston AL   MORE 18 May 1841
    daughter of Masse Bassett of Providence RI died
    at the National Hotel. With husband and baby on
    their way to visit her parents. Episcopal.

GEE, Amanda wife of Lysander died 22 October age 27.   SWERE 29 Oct 1848

GENTRY, Louise died 31 August in her 29th year. (Wife   PWH 2 Sep 1843
    of George; their son James died 26 August.)
    Resident of Shelby Co.

GENTRY, Mary Jane, oldest daughter of Moses died at   PWH 25 Nov 1847
    West Ely 17 Nov. in her 16th year.

GEYER, Mrs. Clara B., consort of H. S., died Thursday
    last.   MORE 3 Nov 1829
    Johanna E., consort of Henry S., Esq., died at   MORE 16 Oct 1837
    the residence of Archibald Gamble 14 October.

GIBBONS, Miss Catherine died 24th inst age 35. Funeral   MORE 25 Jan 1848
    the Cathedral to Catholic cemetery.

GIBSON, Mrs. Ellen, widow of Guian, age 79, died in   MORE 20 Sep 1827
    Lincoln Co. age 79.

GIDDINGS, Mrs. Frances, consort of George of   BOLT 24 July 1841
    Monroe Co., died 20th inst.

GIST, Mary, consort of Robert, died 21st inst. Funeral   MORE 23 Mar 1840
    from residence of Mrs. Wade, #36 wnd St.

GIVENS, Mrs. Sarah, wife of Thomas J., died 2 April   MIN 4 Apr 1835
    near Westport, in Jackson Co.

GLASCOCK, Anne, wife of Asa, late of Farquhar Co. VA   MORE 22 Oct 1823
    died at New London, Ralls Co., 1 October.

GLASGOW, Mrs., wife of Nathan, died in Boone Co.   MIN 15 Mar 1834
    6 March age 29.

GLASS, Martha A., consort of Samuel B., died age 32   MORE 29 Nov 1838
    in Danville, Montgomery Co. 21 Nov. Left
    husband and 2 children.

GLENN, Lavinia, consort of Thomas and daughter of   MORE 23 Sep 1843
    -- Stoddars of Conn., died at Cuivre Creek,
    Montgomery Co., 14 Sep. (BGRAD 23 Sep gives
    name as Levina, age as 37)
    Lucinda, consort of Thomas, died in Montgomery   SALT 12 Dec 1840
    Co. 22 October.

GLENN, Mrs. S., daughter of John Sappington of Gravois settlement, died 17 September.	MORE 3 Oct 1811
GODDARD, Fanny C., wife of A. N., died 25 April in Worcester Mass. age 34.	MORE 21 May 1844
GOODFELLOW, Mrs. Ann of St. Louis died (16 inst?)	MORE 16 Feb 1836
GOODSPEED, Mrs. Eleanor, consort of David, died Tuesday.	MORE 20 July 1837
GORIN, Mrs. Mary wife of Dr. R.B. died in Louisiana MO 10th inst age 35. (MORE 16 Jan :Dr. B. W.)	BGRAD 24 Jan 1846
GRACE, Mrs. Margaret age 56 died 10 November.	SWERE 19 Nov 1848
GRACE, Ann, wife of Pierce Esq. and daughter of Capt. Andrew Harper died in New Orleans " a short time since."	MORE 27 Mar 1846
GRAFTON, Mary L., wife of Gen. J. D. and daughter of Jared Elliott Esq. of Clinton (late Killingworth) Conn., died in Ste. Genevieve 14th inst.	MORE 23 Nov 1838
GRAHAM, Margaret, consort of Dr. __, died of Cholera 23rd inst.	MORE 27 June 1835
GRANT, Ann C. wife of Elijah died age 57. Nashville pc	MORE 27 June 1849
GRAPEVINE, Mary wife of Frederick died 28 January age 28y 10m 11d. Residence Pine-14th St.	MORE 29 Jan 1848
GRAY, Mrs. Eliza, wife of Dr. John B. and daughter of Col. J. D. Learned of Burlington, Iowa Ter., died yesterday in her 21st year. Funeral from residence of her brother-in-law Dr. Adreen Corn. Paris KY and Burlington IA pc.	MORE 25 Apr 1841
GREEN, Mrs. Asenath, consort of Elder Th. P., pastor of Baptist church, died at Cape Girardeau in her 33rd year.	BOLT 14 Nov 1840 MORE 10 Nov 1840
GREEN, Lucy Ann, wife of Willis M., died 3rd inst. (They had been married about two weeks.)	MIN 12 Oct 1827
GREEN, Catherine, consort of James, formerly of Wheeling, VA died 6th inst at the home of her son-in-law William Harsha. Resided 7th St. north of Franklin. Methodist cemetery.	MORE 7 Oct 1841
GREEN, Nancy, wife of David, engineer, died Wednesday evening last. Resided 8th St. near Franklin. (Her husband had been killed in the explosion of the Persian on 14 November.)	MORE 10 Nov 1840
GREGORY, Ann, wife of Joseph W., died age 37. Resided 115 8th St. New York pc	MORE 29 June 1849
GRISMORE, Mrs. Sarah consort of Nathan died 20 Dec.	SWERE 22 Dec 1845
GRISWOLD, Mrs. Ann, wife of M. W. and daughter of John O'Hannon, died at her father's home in Franklin Co. 4th inst. Left baby son.	MORE 16 Mar 1842
GROOM, Mrs. -- wife of Abraham died 7 April in Clay Co. Formerly of Howard Co.	MIN 14 Apr 1826

GUARDHOUSE, Mrs. Ellen, wife of Frederick, died   MORE 30 Nov 1830
          Sunday evening last.

GUIBORD, Ursa died at Ste. Genevieve in her 71st year.   MORE 26 Oct 1843
          Mary Ursula died at Ste. Genevieve 26th ult   MORE 4 Oct 1843
          age 16y 5m.

GUION, Mrs. Felicite died at Carondelet 24th inst   MORE 26 Feb 1841
          in her 37th year. Wife of J. B. Delisle.

GUION, Mrs. Josephe relict of the late Robert died   MORE 17 Jan 1844
          yesterday. Funeral from her residence, 2nd
          & Poplar, to the Cathedral.

HAIGHT, Mary Ann, wife of Fletcher M. Esq., died   MORE 13 Jan 1848
          Tuesday 11 Jan. Funeral from Presbyterian Ch.

HALDERMAN, Mrs. Susan Henderson died at Alton 17th   MORE 24 Dec 1836
          inst, consort of Dr. John J. Formerly
          of Chariton.

HALE, Mrs. Lucinda A., consort of George B., died   MORE 12 Oct 1843
          Saturday. Residence 7th & Market.

HALL, Eliza A. B., sister of Charles, died yesterday,   MORE 25 Jan 1837
          in her 43rd year.   "   23 Jan   "

HALL, Eliza Jane, daughter of Major John, died 19 Oct.   SLINQ 8 Nov 1823
          at Herculaneum age 15.

HALL, Miss Mildred died 6th inst in her 26th year.   BOLT 12 Mar 1842

HALL, Sarah, wife of D. W. and daughter of William   MORE 14 Jan 1849
          Smith, formerly of Sutten, Mass., died 13th
          inst. Funeral from residence of J. W. Owings
          to the Episcopal cemetery.

HALL, Sarah died at Glasgow 10 Dec. in her 18th year.   BOLT 1 Apr 1843

HALLEY, Mrs. Ann, consort of P. W., died 28 Jan. Left   BOLT 3 Feb 1844
          husband, 3 sons, 2 daughters.

HALSTEAD, Mrs. Letty, relict of the late Daniel, died   BOLT 12 Dec 1840
          at the residence of her son-in-law Lewis
          Bumgardner. Formerly of Lexington KY.

HAMILTON, Martha Ann consort of Charles died 10th inst   PWH 19 July 1843
          in West Ely in her 20th year.

HAMILTON, Susan died at the residence of U. Raisin   MORE 28 Sep 1841
          27 Sept. age about 75.

HAMMOND, Nancy died 24th ult at the residence of John   MORE 9 Oct 1845
          Anderson in Jefferson Co., in her 67th year.

HAMMOND, Susan, wife of John R., died yesterday. Funeral MORE 6 July 1842
          from her residence on Collins St.

HAMMOND, Jane, wife of the late William, died yesterday. MORE 18 Dec 1848
          Resided at 128 Carr.

HANENKAMP, Julia, consort of R. P., died at Glasgow   MODE 31 Aug 1846
          last Tuesday of pulmonary affection.

28

HANNAH, Jane, wife of Samuel Esq. of Boone Co., died 24 April.	COP 30 Apr 1842
HARBAUGH, Narcissa Wilson wife of Perry died 27th inst in her 25th year. Resided on Florida near Main.	MORE 28 Feb 1848
HARDEN, Mrs. Mary died in St. Louis Friday last.	MORE 22 Nov 1831
HARDING, Josephine youngest daughter of Joseph died in her 25th year. Resident of Central Twp. Funeral from St. Francis Xavier Church.	MORE 4 July 1846
HARLEY, Hanah died 30 Dec. age 75, a native of Belfast, Antrim, Ireland.	COMB 31 Dec 1846
HARRIS, Mrs. -- died Monday evening last.	MORE 22 Sep 1819
HARRIS, Mrs. --, wife of Capt., died of cholera.	MORE 6 Nov 1832
HARRIS, Mrs. Margaret died Monday last.	MOAR 12 June 1835
HARRIS, Mrs. Mary A. R., consort of Dr. Moses S., late of Scott Co. MO, died 25 August. "Wife, sister, friend"	MORE 4 Sep 1839
HARRIS, Minerva C., wife of C. R. Esq., recently of Columbia, died 20 March age 26.	COP 26 Mar 1842
HARRIS, Margaret Shelby, relict of Oliver Sr., died in Cape Girardeau 25th ult age 72. Formerly of Mecklenburg Co. NC, moved to Cape in 1820.	MORE 11 Oct 1844
HARRISON, Maria Louisa wife of James died in St. Louis 4 February.	BRUNS 17 Feb 1849
Interred Episcopal cemetery. Resided at 8th & Gratiot.	SWERE 12 Feb 1849
HART, Mrs. Allen died near Glasgow.	BRUNS 2 Aug 1849
HARTSHORN, Sarah Jane consort of Lewis Augustus died 13 March in her 21st year. Daughter of Thomas Cohen. Funeral St. John's Church.	MORE 14 Mar 1843
HARTWELL, Mary Charlotte, consort of Benjamin, died 20th inst age 18. Daughter of Dr. John W. Hayes. "Husband, parents, friends."	STGAZ 24 Oct 1845
HARVEY, Mrs., consort of John, died Monday last.	BOLT 8 Jan 1841
HARVY, Mrs. Eliza, died 29 Oct. Methodist. Left "many relatives."	BOLT 4 Nov 1843
HARVEY, Rebecca, consort of James E., Esq., died 13th inst. Youngest daughter of Maj. George B. Tolson	MODE 25/23 Aug 1847 " 30 Aug 1847
HASCALL, Martha daughter of Maj. E. N. died 5th inst Saverton, Ralls Co. age 19 "of the prevailing epidemic"	FREEP 20 June 1833
Prudence P., consort of Maj. E. N., died 3rd inst. at Saverton, Ralls Co.	MORE 12 Sep 1837
HASE, Elizabeth widow of Frederick C. died near Perryville 29th ult in her 72nd year.	SLDU 19 Aug 1846

HASSENGER, Wilhelmina, wife of William, died in West Ely   PWH 21 Oct 1847
    4th inst in her 32nd year. Left 4 children.

HASTIE, Elizabeth Ann, wife of Thomas F., Clark Co.,   MORE 19 Nov 1842
    died 27th ult age 32. Left 3-day-old infant.

HATFIELD, Susan M., wife of Rev. E. F., died in St.   MIN 14 Mar 1835
    Louis 22 Feb.   MORE 24 Feb 1835

HATHAWAY, Margaret, wife of A. B., died at Weston   MODE 22 Feb 1848
    Wednesday last age 22y 10m.

HAWKINS, Margaret consort of Joseph died Thursday last.   PWH 14 Oct 1843

HAWLEY, Delia Jane consort of Orestes K. and daughter   PWH 19 Aug 1843
    of the Rev. John Bartlett of Avon, Conn. died
    11th inst.

HAWLEY, Mrs. Jane B. died at Palmyra 11 August. (same?)   PWH 7 Oct 1843

HAYDEN, Almina Eaton, wife of David Esq. and daughter   MORE 18 Oct 1848
    of the late Gen. William Eaton of Mass. died,
    fineral from Planter's House.

HAYDON, Mrs. John G. and child died of cholera at   MORE 28 June 1833
    Palmyra.

HAYDEN, Mrs. Penina wife of Dr. James R. died 25 Oct.   BGRAD 4 Nov 1843
    age 31. Formerly of Marion Co. KY. Left two
    sons and a daughter. Catholic.

HAYS, Mrs. Elizabeth wife of John B. died at West Ely   PWH 28 Sep 1848
    13th inst. Formerly of Fayette Co. KY. Presbyterian.

HAYS, Mrs. Mary L., consort of Dr. John B., died in   BOLT 24 Apr 1841
    Monroe Co. 16th inst.

HAYWOOD, Mrs. Amanda consort of R. J. died 27th ult   SALT 10 July 1841
    at Clarksville in her 22nd year.

HAZZARD, Sally consort of Henry H. died 3 May age 46.   MIN 3 July 1830

HEAD, Miss Sarah, second daughter of Dr. Waller of   BOLT 26 Feb 1842
    Huntsville, Randolph Co. died Saturday last.

HEATH, Sarah B., consort of Dr. William, died yesterday   MORE 17 Apr 1844
    in her 71st year. Member of Centenary Methodist
    Church. Methodist 55 years. Petersburg and
    Lynchburg VA pc.

HEBERT, Mme. Agnesse died 21 March in her 70th year.   MORE 9 Apr 1814

HEMPSTEAD, Mrs. Rachel wife of Charles S. Esq. died   MORE 3 Dec 1823
    28 October age 28.

HEMPSTEAD, Mrs. Eliza died Wednesday of cholera.   MORE 30 Oct 1832

HEMPSTEAD, Mrs. --, consort of Stephen, died in St.   MORE 21 June 1833
    Charles on Wednesday last.

HEMPSTEAD, Sarah Augusta, consort of William, died   MORE 20 Aug 1844
    at Galena IL age 29.

HENDERSON, Mrs. Jane, consort of George, died in St.   MORE 25 Oct 1839
    Louis 23 Oct. "Numerous circle of friends."

HENDERSON, Miss Louisa, daughter of John of Concord, this   FULT 9 Feb 1849
    county, died 29th ult.

HENRY, Ann C., wife of Dr. Julis, died 13th inst. Funeral   MORE 14 Apr 1846
    from residence, Walnut-7th St.

HERNDON, Mrs. Catherine died 27th ult.   INJN 10 Oct 1844

HERNDON, Mrs. --, wife of Dr. H. of Randolph, hanged   BOLT 16 May 1846
    herself on 6 May.

HERRICK, Mrs. Ann W., consort of Maj. E. B., died at   MORE 1 Feb 1831
    Fredericktown on 25 Janurary last, leaving a
    small daughter.

HERRING, Mrs. Nancy, consort of William and daughter   BRUNS 9 Dec 1848
    of Asa Turner, died Wednesday.

HICKMAN, Rachel, consort of William, died 7 August in   PWH 12 Aug 1843
    her 65th year. Methodist.

HIGGINS, Elizabeth died 26 December, relict of the   SWERE 29 Dec 1845**
    late William.

HIGGINS, Margaret died 23rd inst at the residence   MORE 28 July 1846
    of her son G. W. in Bonhomme Twp. Consort
    of Augustus C. of Montgomery Co. MD

HIGGINS, Mrs. Elizabeth, widow of William, died   MORE 27 Dec 1845 **
    26 December age 70. Residence near Patterson,
    #62 4th St. Catholic cemetery.

HILBERT, Sarah Ann, wife of A. Z., died 14 January at   MORE 25 Jan 1840
    Petty (Peity? Perry?) Mills MO. Left baby son.

HILL, Mrs. --, consort of David B., died Thursday.   MORE 24 Apr 1832

HILL, Fanny, wife of William, died last Wednesday.   MORE 31 Jan 1825

HILL, Frances A., consort of Dr. William C., died in   BRUNS 21 June 1849
    25th year Sunday last. Left 3 children.

HINCH, Charity, widow of Samuel, died in Howard Co.   MIN 5 Mar 1831
    31 January age 75.

HIX, Mrs. Nancy, relict of Archibald, died age 68.   BRUNS 14 Oct 1847
    Daughter of Jacob & Elizabeth Woodson of Prince
    Edward Co., VA; to Missouri in 1819. Baptist.

HIX, Sarah, consort of Ottoway B., daughter of Charles   BOLT 1 Jan 1842
    Talbot, died 25th ult in her 30th year. Left
    husband and children. Lynchburg VA pc

HODGE, Mrs. -- died in Louisiana MO 17th inst.   BGRAD 21 Oct 1843

HOFLAND, Mrs. -- died recently age 73.   SWERE 23 Dec 1844

HOLLAND, Mrs. Elizabeth, consort of William, of   BRUNS 8 July 1848
    Keytesville, died Saturday age about 50.

HOLLAND, Mrs. Henry died near Keytesville 4th inst.   BOLT 14 Aug 1841
    Wife and mother of 3, all "age of maturity."

HOLLYMAN, Elizabeth P, daughter of John, died 23rd   PWH 26 Feb 1845
    inst in her 19th year.

HOLMES, Mrs. A. P. died 22 May age 35.   MORE 30 May 1849

HONORE, Mrs. Polly died at her residence about 10 miles   MORE 4 Apr 1821
  from St. Louis on 30 March. Consort of Michael
  Tesson Honore. Left a large family.

HOOTON, Mrs. Enoch Esq. died Tuesday last leaving a   PWH 12 Mar 1848
  large family.

HOPKINS, Frances G., consort of William H., died in   MORE 19 Dec 1835
  St. Louis Wednesday night last.
  Mary, sister of Maj. Wm. H., died 5 Dec.   MORE 20 Dec 1838
  in Cincinnati in her 61st year.

HOPSON, Caroline H., consort of Dr. Winthrop H.,   BRUNS 27 Sep 1849
  died in Fayette 20 September in her 27th year.

HOPSON, Mrs. Ann H., wife of Lieut. John D., died   MORE 7 Dec 1826
  at Cantonment Adams near St. Louis 2 Dec. age 23.

HORINE, Mrs. Margaret consort of Jacob died 9th inst   MORE 16 Feb 1820
  in Jefferson Co.

HORN, Mary F. consort of Charles W. died 4th inst.   MORE 5 Feb 1849
  age 29. Residence 2nd & O'Fallon. Quincy and
  Burlington pc.

HOSSLEBACK, Sarah Ann, wife of George, died 20 December   MORE 23 Dec 1844
  at the home of her father J. Herding in
  St. Louis Co. Formerly of Frederick Co. MD

HOWE, Jennet wife of Dr. Cheney died 7th inst.   MORE 8 Dec 1847
  of consumption.

HOWELL, Elizabeth M., consort of John M. of Carrollton,   BRUNS 2 Aug 1849
  died 26th inst in her 22nd year. One child.

HOWELL, Margaret A., wife of Maj. W. W., died at   PWH 2 Aug 1849
  Paris MO 17th inst.

HOWELL, Maria Louisa, consort of William G., died near   PWH 9 Sep 1847
  Paris MO 1st inst age 26y 10m 13d. Left 6
  small children.

HOXEY, wife of Rev. died in Fulton last Wednesday.   MIN 7 Apr 1832

HUBBARD, Mrs. Elizabeth age 70 died 16 December at   MORE 5 May 1829
  residence in St. Ferdinand Twp.

HUBBARD, Mrs. Mary C., wife of E. H., died at Osceola,   MORE 9 Sep 1844
  St. Clair Co. MO 22 July. Formerly of
  Philadelphia.

HUGHES, Mrs. E. died Monday evening last, native of   JINQ 24 July 1845
  Virginia. Methodist.

HUGHES, Mrs. Jane, wife of Richard, died age 32.   MIN 27 Feb 1824

HUGHES, Letitia D., consort of Leander, died 1st   PLAT 5 Jan 1849
  inst in Platte Co. age 52. Baptist 20 years.

HUGHES, Mrs. Martha, relict of the late William, died   BOLT 9 Oct 1841
  at her Mansion House 30 September age 74.

HUGHES, Mrs. Nancy, consort of James, died 3 November.   BOLT 13 Nov 1841

HUGHES, Rebecca, consort of Thomas, died 31 January age 32. — SWERE 7 Feb 1848

HULL, Louisa Ann, consort of William C. of St. Louis, died at the residence of her father Rev. D. C. Banks in Louisville KY 2nd inst. — MORE 16 Feb 1836
    Mary L., wife of William C. of St. Louis, daughter of the late Talcott Banks MD of New York, died in New York 18 Nov. — MORE 1 Dec 1846

HUNT, Mrs. Josephine S., consort of Philemon of St. Louis, died 13th inst at Lexington KY where she had gone for her health. — MORE 24 Apr 1834

HUNT, Julia, wife of Lieut. Samuel W. of the 3rd Reg. Inf., died 2 October age 26. — MORE 5 Oct 1826

HUNT, Mrs., widow of Thomas, died at Bellefontaine yesterday. — MORE 25 Jan 1809

HUNTER, Mrs. Ann died at the home of her daughter Mrs. Smith 21st inst in her 79th year. — PWH 25 June 1845

HUNTER, Lucy, consort of the late James, died at Mobile, AL where she had gone to improve her health. Left a small son and daughter. She had been a resident of Scott Co. — SMAD 23 Mar 1838

HUNTER, Martha, daughter of James, died 28th inst age 31. — JEFRE 31 Oct 1840

HUNTER, Mrs. Martha, consort of Maj. W. C., formerly a merchant of St. Louis, died at Alton "some time since." — MORE 27 Oct 1819

HUNTINGTON, Mrs. Naomi, died at the house of Jonas Seely near Albyville 5th inst., wife of Ebenezer Esq. and youngest daughter of Reuben Runyan of Frankfort KY. In the 19th year of her age. — MORE 8 Sep 1819

HURST, Hester B., wife of John B., died Tuesday evening age 26. — PWH 10 Aug 1848

HUTCHINSON, Agnes, consort of Asa, died Friday 13th inst age 29y 1m 8d. Funeral from residence, Mound & 2nd. — MORE 14 Aug 1841

HUTCHERSON, Margaret daughter of John died in Lewis Co. 20 Dec. in her 18th year. Pneumonia. — PWH 1 Jan 1846

HUTT, Mrs. Judith consort of Thomas G. died near Troy 24 September. — BGDB 27 Sep 1845

HYATT, Maria, wife of Frederick Esq., died in St. Louis Co. 12th inst. — MORE 15 June 1839
    Mrs. Ann G., consort of Frederick, died in Jefferson City 1 Feb. — MORE 5 Feb 1845

HYDE, Johannah, wife of William, died in her 43rd year. Residence Franklin Ave. Catholic Cemetery. — MORE 24 Sep 1847

IJAMS, Miss Frances R. died Tuesday last in St. Joseph in her 13th year.	STGAZ 4 Oct 1845
INGRAM, Mary, consort of Capt., died of cholera 7 miles from Brunswick Monday, age about 40.	BRUNS 31 May 1849
INGRAHAM, Mrs. Stephen of Schuyler Co. and her six children were killed in a fire 22 April.	PWH 13 May 1847
IRVINE, Julie, wife of William, Esq. died yesterday in her 26th year. Funeral from her residence above the Big Mound. Presbyterian burying ground.	MORE 27 Mar 1843
JACARD, Adelle, wife of Lewis, died 16th inst age 38. Resided 102 Myrtle. Interred Presbyterian Burying Ground on St. Charles Road.	MORE 17 Dec 1848
JACKSON, Mrs. Jane, wife of R., native of England, died at Prairietown in October, 1846. Left children, one the wife of Edward Turner of St. Louis.	SWERE 25 Jan 1847
JACKSON, Margaret, was murdered near Creve Coeur Lake. George Van Leer arrested.	MORE 20 Apr 1841
JACKSON, Mrs. Mary died at the residence of her son-in-law G. P. Bass of the Fayette vicinity on 7th inst in her 79th year. Emigrated from KY in 1828 with her husband Thomas. A Baptist for 30 years.	MODE 18/16 Mar 1846
JACKSON, Mrs. Mary, consort of James, Sr., died 31st ult in her 70th year. Baptist 45 years.	MODE 14/12 Apr 1847
JACOBI, Susan M., consort of John C., died 15th inst in her 41st year. Resided 162 S. 3rd. Interred Christ Church burying ground. NY, Washington pc.	MORE 16 June 1849
JAMERSON, Miss Mary Ann died of cholera in Palmyra.	MORE 28 June 1833
JAMES, Mrs. Sarah, consort of W. J. and daughter of William Jenkins, died 25th ult.	SPAD 11 Mar 1845
JAYNE, Mrs. Keturah of this city died 3rd inst. Consort of Dr. Z. Boonville & Knoxville TN pc.	MORE 10 June 1842
JEFFERSON, Mrs. M. A. of Jefferson City died at the residence of Josiah Hodge in Osage Co. 9th inst in her 20th year.	JINQ 10 Oct 1844
JEFFRIES, Eliza Julia wife of Robert A. and daughter of the late Henry Fackley died at Union, Franklin Co. age 19y 11m 2d. (MORE 1 May says Henry Fackler, gives age 19y 11m 12d)	BGRAD 11 May 1844
JEFFREY, Ann Eliza wife of Jacob died 6 January age 36y 9m. Resided 3rd & Hansel.	MORE 7 Jan 1848
JEFFRIES, Mrs. Narcissa, consort of Coleman, died in the Brunswick neighborhood in her 53rd year. 14th inst. Came from Virginia several years ago. Baptist 35 years. (A daughter died in April 1849)	BRUNS 27 Jan ? (1849)

JENKINS, Sinah murdered at Jefferson Barracks; James   MORE 20 July 1830
    Jenkins, a discharged soldier, charged with
    the murder. (She was also called Sinah Brooks.)

JENKINSON, Mrs. Ann, late matron of the Orphan's Home,   SWERE 30 Apr 1849
    died yesterday.

JETT, Miss Caroline died 15th inst of bilious fever in   MORE 21 Aug 1832
    the 18th year of her age.

JEWELL, Mrs. Cynthia wife of William died in Columbia   MIN 22 Oct 1822
                            Friday last.

JONES, Margaret Arbuckle, relict of Benjamin, died at   MORE 29 Apr 1837
    the residence of her son-in-law Franklin Raborg
    suddenly Friday morning in her 55th year. Funeral
    from Raborg home, #47 St. Charles St., to her
    late residence on Gravois. Lewisburg VA pc.

JONES, Mrs. Eliza, consort of John, died Thursday last.   MORE 15 Sep 1819

JONES, Mrs. Elizabeth died 15th inst in her 92nd year.   BOLT 22 Apr 1843

JONES, Elizabeth, consort of John Knight Jones, died   MORE 10 Nov 1838
    in Fredericktown 31 Oct. in her 41st year.
    Daughter of the late Joseph Leentee.

JONES, Mary died at the home of her son Gen. Augustus   MORE 18 Jan 1839
    at Potosi 6th inst in her 75th year.

JONES, Melvina, consort of Dr. Samuel J., died 27 Nov.   STGAZ 7 Jan 1848
    in her 18th year. Left an infant.

JONES, Mrs. Nancy E., consort of Rev. William W. and   JINQ 28 Aug 1845
    daughter of Samuel & Isabella Moore, died 14 July.
    Born near Cynthiana KY.

JONES, Mrs. Parmela, relict of Robert, formerly of   MORE 28 Mar 1838
    Lynchburg VA, died at Hannibal 20 (or 28)
    February at the home of her son-in-law Robert
    Briggs. Presbyterian.

JONES, Susan, wife of William, age 47, died 21 September   JEFRE 5 Oct 1833
    of cholera. Left a large family of children.

JONES, Laura, consort of Theodore Esq., died 8 May   PWH 18 May 1848
    in St. Louis. (Apparently from Marion Co.)

JONES, Mrs. --, died at the residence of her son   PWH 16 Sep 1847
    William in Round Grove Twp. Friday at a very
                            advanced age.

JUDEN, Mrs. Eliza S., consort of John, clerk of the   INP 31 Aug 1822
    Circuit Court, died 19th inst.

JUDSON, Mrs. Edithar, wife of S. P., died in St. Louis   MORE 24 Jan 1832
    of consumption on 17 January.

JOHNSON, Mrs. --, died Friday last age about 50.   BRUNS 16 Aug 1849

JOHNSTONE, Charlotte L., consort of Peter W., died   MORE 26 Aug 1842
    yesterday. Funeral from her residence, 88
    Elm St. (between 4th & 5th).

35

JOHNSON, Mrs. Elizabeth died 29th ult in her 74th year.   BOLT 5 Oct 1844

JOHNSTON, Henriette P., consort of A. Sidney, late of   SCOMB 21 Aug 1835
the U. S. Army, died 12 August at the
residence of George Hancock, Esq. near
Louisville.

JOHNSON, Neville, wife of Julius D. Esq., died 21st inst   MORE 22 Feb 1844
age 31. Lynchburg VA & Richmond Whig pc.

JOHNSON, Mary Elizabeth daughter of Philip C. of New   MORE 17 Apr 1845
York died at the home of Dr. R. F. Barrett at
the age of 19.

JOHNSON, Mary Ann, eldest daughter of Richard H. and   BGRAD 31 Dec 1842
Louisa, died 27 December of a protracted
indisposition. Age 24y 1m 1d.

KELLY, Miss --, drowned in the Osage River 15 miles   BRUNS 26 Jan 1848
below Warsaw.

KELLY, Anna T., wife of Eugene, died 28th inst in her   MORE 29 June 1848
27th year. Resided 8th & Pine.

KELLY, Margaret died 13th inst in her 22nd year.   SLDU 14 Sep 1846
Funeral from res. of her brother John, 11th
& Green.

KELLY, Mrs. Nancy, consort of John, died at the   WEM 12 Sep 1839
residence of her father Jesse Davis in Saline
Co. 3 September. Sister, daughter, wife, in
her 23rd year. Methodist.

KELLY, Susan, consort of William, died Saturday.   PWH 13 Aug 1845

KELLY, Catherine and two children; death shown on   MORE 20 June 1840
hospital list. Native of Ireland. Late of
St. Peters. Wife of soldier.

KELLY, Mary and infant, died in the hospital. Born   MORE 20 June 1840
in Ireland, age 23; late of Shawneetown IL.

KEMPER, Mrs. Caroline died 27 June; her two daughters   PWH 20 July 1843
died about the same time, Isabelle (13) on
22 June and Amanda (11) 23 June.

KEMPER, Susanna, wife of Enoch Esq. died 18 September.   MIN 27 Sep 1827
Funeral service for the wife and daughter of   MIN 29 Aug 1828
Enoch to be preached the first Sunday in
September by Rev. J. Williams.

KENNEDY, Sarah Ann of St. Louis died in New York   SWERE 29 Oct 1848
18 October, Cincinnati & Mobile pc.

KENNEDY, Sarah M., consort of Henry, died in Hannibal   MORE 20 Oct 1840
in her 29th year. Formerly of Rochester NY.

KENNEDY, Mrs. -- died Saturday last at the house of her   MORE 11 Jan 1844
father Lewis E. Martin near Bridgeton.

KENNETT, Martha Ann Eliza wife of L. N. died 29 August   MORE 5 Sep 1835
at Farmington. Left 2-year-old daughter.

KERR, Mrs. --, wife of W. D., died 24th inst.   JEFRE 26 Sep 1840
      Formerly of Virginia.

KERR, Mrs. James, died 17th inst.   BGRAD 3 June 1843

KERR, Eliza, wife of John, died in St. Louis   MORE 7 June 1833
      Wednesday evening last.

KETCHUM, Rebecca, relict of Maj. Daniel, died at   MORE 10 Dec 1835
      Jefferson Barracks 6th inst ae 54 y 8m.

KEYTE, Mrs. Rebecca died 27th ult age 83. Born Colton,   BRUNS 1 July 1848
      Staffordshire, Eng., mother of the late James
      Keyte. Methodist.

KIBBY, Mrs., wife of Col. Amos, died in Montgomery Co.   STCHMO 19 Aug 1820
      7th inst.

KINCAID, Sister Antoinette of the Sisters of St.   MORE 15 May 1848
      Joseph died 14th inst in her 26th year.

KING, Mrs. William, of Fulton, was recently murdered   SWERE 22 July 1844
      by a black servant girl.

KING, Eliza Ann, wife of Wyllys, formerly of Hartford,   MORE 9 July 1840
      Conn. died 6 July age 35.

KING, Mrs. Maria, wife of Baldwin of Union, MO died   MORE 5 Jan 1836
      in St. Louis Tuesday evening last.

KINGSBURY, Julie A., consort of Lt. James W., USA   MORE 17 Mar 1836
      and daughter of J. P. Cabanne, died
      yesterday.

KIRBY, Mrs. Martha, wife of F. F., died in Boone Co.   COP 16 Apr 1842
      2 April age 31.

KNOUS, Mrs., consort of Henry, Sr., died near Franklin   BOLT 29 Aug 1840
      21st inst at an advanced age.

KNIGHT, Mrs. Emeline G., died yesterday as a result   MORE 31 Aug 1843
      of a gas lamp explosion, in her 28th year.
      New Hampshire *Sentinel* pc. Resided on
      Myrtle between 3rd & 4th Sts.

KNOX, Olivia, wife of Reuben, MD of St. Louis died   MORE 22 Mar 1839
      in Kinaton NC on Friday, 1st inst.

KREIGER, Sophia, wife of J. Philip, died 16th inst.   MORE 17 June 1849
      Resided Theater Alley.

LA BEAUME, Joyce B., daughter of Samuel and Ann   PWH 18 Oct 1849
      Vandiver, died in Shelby Co. 7 Sept. in
      her 39th year. Left husband and one son.
      Formerly of Hampshire Co. VA.

LA BEAUME, Mrs. Susan, died at the residence of her son   MORE 12 Feb 1844
      in New Orleans 1st inst age 63. Relict of
      Louis T.

LAFFERTY, Amanda, consort of Daniel, died 26th inst   JEFRE 30 June 1838
      of typhus fever age 18. Left husband and
      small family of children. Lately from NY.

LAFON, Elizabeth, consort of Richard and daughter of Mrs. Elizabeth Hatcher, died 27th ult. in Lewis Co. in her 31st year. Left 5 children. — PWH 1 Apr 1847

LAJOIE, Mrs. --, died Thursday last age 107 years. — MORE 3 Aug 1830

LAKNAN (LAKENAN), Sarah, consort of James of St. Louis, died 13 July age 38. Native of Virginia. — SLINQ 22 July 1824

LAMOREUX, Adele, wife of Antoine, was found dead in bed 7 August. Funeral from her residence, Poplar and 3rd Sts. — MORE 7 Aug 1846

LAMPKIN, Eviline, wife of Josiah, died yesterday. — JEFRE 9 July 1842

LAMPTON, Eveline, drowned Sunday last, daughter of widow Elizabeth Lampton. — STCHMO 5 Sep 1821

LANDREVILLE, Mrs. Marie Louise, wife of Andre, died a few days ago. — MORE 26 Mar 1814

LANDREVILLE, Mrs. Marie, died 10th inst ae 64y 2m. — MORE 12 Jan 1846

LANE, Anne E., wife of Dr. Hardage, died in her 43rd year. Daughter of Maj. Charles Carroll of NY. — MORE 18 Aug 1846

LANE, Mrs. Frances T., consort of the late G. W., died 15th inst. Formerly of Fairfax Co. VA — PWH 16 Oct 1844

LANE, Virginia died of cholera in Palmyra. — MORE 28 June 1833

LANGHAM, Elizabeth, consort of Maj. E.T., died yesterday age 41. Funeral from residence of William Risley, #70 S. Main. — MORE 7 Aug 1843

LANGLY, MRS.-- died 26th ult., age about 80. — FULT 6 July 1849

LANHAM, Julia H., daughter of Edward and Martha A., died 28 February age 16 y. — SWERE 9 Mar 1846

LAVEILLE, Lavinia, relict of the late Joseph, died 9th inst. Funeral from residence at Elm and Myrtle. — MORE 10 Nov 1848

LAVEILLE, Josephine, daughter of the late Joseph C., died at the residence of Lawrison Riggs, age 24 y. 2m. — MORE 3 Jan 1849

LAVEILLE, Mrs. Elizabeth, consort of Col. Joseph C., died Wednesday last. — MORE 17 Oct 1834

LAWLESS, Paulina Louise, daughter of L.E. and Virginia, died 25th inst age 16y 6m. (She was their only surviving child.) — MORE 28 June 1843

LAWRENCE, Mehitable, wife of George and daughter of Samuel Morrison, died at St. Joseph 28 April. — PWH 10 May 1849

LAY, Mary, consort of Daniel Jr., died 26th ult in her 30th year. — BOLT 6 June 1846

LAYTON, Mrs. --, recently murdered by her husband in Perry Co. (He was apprehended.) — MORE 20 Feb 1841

LEAR, Susan, daughter of John decd., died of typhoid 27 December.	PWH 13 Jan 1848
LEAR, Nancy, cinsort of William B., died at West Ely in her 45th year.	PWH 25 Nov 1847
LEAR, Elizabeth Ann, consort of Zachariah, died in Shelby Co. 30 January. Daughter of Wm. Elgin of Loudoun Co. VA, reared by her uncle Peter Rust and his wife. Left a 10-m-old son.	PWH 19 Feb 1842
LEAR, Mary, consort of Zachariah and daughter of the late Samuel Pool, died 20th inst in her 36th y.	PWH 7 Oct 1847
LeBEAU, Mme., died age 64. Funeral from Cathedral to the Catholic cemetery.	MORE 2 Nov 1843
LEDGWICK, Mrs. Sarah, consort of Mr. S., died yesterday. Funeral from residence, Green St. near 6th.	MORE 15 May 1841
LEE, Catherine M., age about 45, died at the residence of Oliver Harris 16th inst. New Orleans and Philadelphia pc.	MORE 20 Dec 1848
LEE, Mrs. Jane died Thursday at the residence of her son Thomas, age 66.	SWERE 3 Aug 1846
LEE, Mrs. Mary Ann, died 10 July at the residence of Jesse G. Lindell in St. Louis Co., age 70.	SWERE 17 July 1848
LEE, Mrs. Mary, wife of Thomas, died Friday last.	MORE 16 Mar 1830
LEEPER, Florence, died 17th inst age 83. Born in VA, emigrated first to KY and to MO 12 years ago. Member Associated Reformed Church.	FULT 22 Sep 1848
LEFFINGWELL, Laura Simmons, wife of Hiram. Interred Episcopal cemetery.	MORE 29 May 1849
LEHMAN, Mrs. Elizabeth, consort of John P., died Sunday. Funeral from residence, South 2nd St. near the bridge.	MORE 1 Feb 1841
LEINTZ, Mrs., daughter of Alphonso Wetmore of St. Louis, died in Boone Co. 12th inst. She was just home from visiting her father, who died 13th inst. (MORE 18 June 1849 spells the name Luntz, gives her name as Calpurnia, her husband's as Montgomery, and says she died at Locust Grove.) See also Lientz.	BRUNS 21 June 1849
LEONARD, ---ssa Bowker, wife of Henry; resided at 45 S. Main. NY and Boston pc.	MORE 29 June 1849
LEONARD, Mary Martha, Sister of Charity, native of Ireland, died age 28.	MORE 4 May 1847
LESPERANCE, Eliza R. Duchoquette, wife of J.B., died Sunday 29th inst.	MORE 31 July 1838
LEWIS, Mrs. John, murdered. Her husband tried but found not guilty.	MORE 11 Feb 1849

LEWIS, Mary Ann, age about 12, died at the residence of Gen. John H. Curd 11 February.	PWH 13 Feb 1841
LIENTZ, Harriet L., youngest daughter of William Esq. of Boone Co., died 20 May in Franklin, age 16.	MIN 24 May 1827
LIGHT, Julia daughter of Rufus C. died Saturday last in Hannibal.	PWH 17 May 1849
Julia T., daughter of Rev. George C., died at Hannibal 12th inst in her 20th year.	BRUNS 24 May 1849
(Probably the latter is correct. Rev. George C. Lewis had a daughter Susan who died in St. Louis in 1840 age 3½.)	
LINDSEY, Julia Ann wife of Nimrod died in Calumet Twp. 10 October.	BGRAD 9 Nov 1844
LINN, Jane Ann, eldest daughter of Hon. Lewis, died in Cincinnati 19th ult at the home of Charles Neave.	MORE 21 June 1836
(COMB 22 June gives death date as 29 May)	
LITTLE, Mrs. Marie Antoinette, wife of John, merchant, died after a long and painful illness.	MORE 20 Feb 1818
LITTLE, Maria, wife of James A., died 30 Sept. age 30.	MORE 3 Oct 1844
LITTLE, Mary Ann, wife of F., died Monday age 45. Hagerstown MD pc.	SWERE 25 Oct 1847
LITTLEJOHN, Elizabeth, wife of Dr. Camuel H. of the US Army, died 7 September at Cantonment Bellefontaine.	MORE 13 Sep 1824
LITTLETON, --, wife of Capt. M, died "lately" in the sinking of the steamboat Eliza. Her body was found near the mouth of the Ohio and was brought to St. Louis for burial. Funeral from her residence, 6th between Franklin and Morgan. Episcopal cemetery.	MORE 2 Nov 1842
LIVESAY, Mrs. Amandy, wife of Joseph, formerly of Greenbrier Co. VA, died Thursday last ae 21. (Her infant son Joseph died Sunday ae 7 d.)	LEXP 30 July 1844
LOCKWOOD, Jane, wife of Richard of St. Louis and daughter of James Morrison of St. Charles, died 13 July in her 26th year. Funeral from residence, St. Charles betweeen 4th & 5th.	MORE 17 July 1848
LOCKWOOD, Ellen, widow of Isaac, died 23rd inst. Resided #505 4th St. (Her husband had died two weeks earlier.) Presbyterian cemetery.	MORE 24 June 1849
LOKER, Mrs. Elizabeth, relict of the late Jacob, died 17th inst in her 54th year.	MORE 21 Aug 1844
LONG, Mrs. Arretta, consort of Joseph, died near Paynesville 20 July in her 42nd year. Left a young family.	SALT 31 July 1841
LONG, Ibby, wife of Thomas, died in Calumet Twp. 27 October.	BGRAD 9 Nov 1844

LONG, Mary Mildred died in St. Louis 27th inst age 77.   SWERE 2 Sep 1844

LONG, Mrs. Nancy died 22nd inst in her 43rd year.   BOLT 27 Sep 1845

LONG, Sarah L. wife of Col. Alton died in St. Louis   SWERE 6 Mar 1848
Co. 12 February age 35.

LONGMIRE, Harriet, wife of Joseph, died 28th ult at   PWH 6 July 1848
the residence of William Longmire.

LONGMIRE, Mrs. William died 19 November.   PWH 26 Nov 1842

LOOMIS, Julia A., wife of Col. G. (US Army) died   SWERE 14 May 1849
9 May age 50. New York, New Haven, and
Vermont, pc.

LOPER, Eliza, consort of James, died Wednesday.   MORE 30 Oct 1832
(During a cholera epidemic.)

LORING, Mrs. J., Mrs. F. and Amanda all died of   MORE 28 June 1833
cholera in Palmyra.

LOUGHLIN, Catherine Foulze, wife of Michael B., died   SWERE 8 Nov 1847
5 November age 17 y 4m. Philadelphia pc.

LOUTHAN, Mary E., daughter of Walker and wife of   PWH 13 Jan 1848
-- Marvin, died of consumption.

LOVELACE, Lucy, wife of Zachariah, died 17th (or 18th)   BGRAD 3 Feb 1844
of pleurisy, 13 hours before the death of
her husband from the same illness. She was
in her 70th year and they had been married
55 years; they were buried in the same grave.
Residents of Hartford Twp. Their son James
died a week later (25 Jan.) at the age of
50, of the same illness.

LOWE, Mrs. Catherine died yesterday age 82. Funeral   MORE 3 May 1838
from the residence of her daughter, Mrs. Samuel
Perry, corner 4th & Walnut.

LOW, Lydia Lucy, daughter of Samuel Davis, Charleston,   MORE 27 Aug 1840
Mass., died Tuesday.

LOWERY, Catherine Agnes, wife of Samuel H. and daughter   SWERE 13 Mar 1848
of Benjamin Clapp, died at the residence of
Laurason Riggs.

LOWRY, Mrs. Malinda, consort of Dr. John J., died   BOLT 16 Mar 1844
Thursday last.

LUCAS, Anna, consort of the Hon. John B. C., a native   MORE 8 Aug 1811
of Normandy, France, died Saturday last.

LUCK, Mrs. Lucy, consort of Asa and daughter of   SALT 10 Apr 1841
Alexander C. Fitzhugh, died age 27 y. Born in
KY, she came to MO with her father. Methodist.
Left 5 children.

LUCKETT (SACKETT?), Mrs. Lucy Ann, consort of Wm. H.,   MORE 8 Dec 1837
died in St. Charles Co. 24 November in her
24th year. Late of Frederick Co. VA.

LYDICK, Elizabeth, wife of Andrew, died in her 68th year. Born in PA, moved to KY, married in her 18th year. Emigrated to MO with her son John. A longtime Methodist. — PWH 17 Sep 1845

LYLE, Mrs. James S. died Thursday last. — MORE 25 Sep 1832

LYNCH, Catherine, wife of William Esq., died in her 36th year yesterday morning. Residence between St. Charles and Washington. Catholic cemetery. — MORE 14 Dec 1840

LYNCH, Mary died 22 November in her 77th year. — MODE 29 Nov 1847

LYONS, Eliza, of the Theatre, died Monday age 28. — SCOMB 27 July 1836

McALISTER, Mrs. Ann consort of David died Tuesday. — SALT 5 June 1841

McARTHUR, Mrs. Frances, native of England, died 30th ult age 61. Residence Olive betw. 3rd-4th. — SWERE 7 Oct 1844

McBRIDE, Mrs. Elizabeth died 23rd inst in her 62nd year. Residence Christy betw. 14th-15th. — MORE 25 Dec 1848

McCABE, Eliza Jane, consort of Dr. J.E. and oldest daughter of the Hon. P. H. McBride, died 3rd inst at the residence of Samuel Harrison Esq. — MORE 13 Apr 1849

McCAMANT, Margaret Thomas, oldest daughter of James and Sarah, died age 14y 1m 4d. — MORE 28 June 1849

McCANN, Mrs. Catherine died yesterday at the Hospital in her 95th year. Formerly of Castle Island, Kerry Co., Ire. Resident of St. Louis 14 years. Catholic cemetery. — MORE 10 Mar 1843

McCARTAN, Maria Louisa, daughter of the late Thomas, died in her 16th year. Residence 4th & Elm. Methodist burying ground. — MORE 12 Sep 1839

McCARTY, Mrs. Ann Maria, consort of Isaac, died at Lexington in her 22nd year, 5th inst. — STGAZ 18 Sep 1846

McCAUSLAND, Mrs. Elizabeth died 19th inst in St. Louis Co. in her 72nd year. — MORE 27 Aug 1846

McCAUSLAND, Mrs. Harriet, wife of John. Funeral from residence, 4th St. Presbyterian cemetery. — MORE 26 Aug 1843

McCENEY, Mrs. Frances C., wife of Henry C., daughter of Col. J.D. Learned, died age 19. Left an 8-day-old daughter (who died in June). Baltimore pc. — MORE 21 Mar 1838

McCLELLAND, Sarah, widow of the late Elisha, died at the residence of her son John A. in her 54th year. Formerly of St. Charles. — MORE 6 Jan 1844

McCLENCHAN, Miss Ann, lately from Louisville, died 14th inst. — MORE 19 July 1831

McCLUER, Margaret Jane, daughter of William, late of Bedford Co. VA, died 31 July in her 16th year. (Her father died the same day.) — MORE 27 Aug 1833

McCLURG, Mrs. Mary died of consumption in St. Louis 21st inst.	MORE 24 Oct 1834.
MacCOLLUM, Dorcas, wife of William, died in Peno (?) Twp. 14th inst. age 19. Tennessee pc.	BGRAD 24 Aug 1844
McCURDY, Mrs. Nancy, consort of Henning B., died near Boonville Thursday 23 March age about 19.	MORE 10 May 1837
McDANIEL, Mrs. Betsy, wife of a soldier, fell from a barge at Bellefontaine 13 September and was drowned.	MORE 2 Oct 1813
McDANIEL, Mary, wife of John, died Saturday. Formerly of Philadelphia.	MORE 10 Jan 1842
McDANIEL, Susan, oldest daughter of William, died Saturday last age 16.	PWH 19 Mar 1846
McDONALD, Mrs. Bridget died Friday last.	MORE 7 Dec 1830
MacDONOUGH, Frances Brenton, wife of Augustus R. and daughter of Edward C. McVicker of Utica, NY died 3 December age 26. Funeral from residence, 6th & Locust.	MORE 5 Dec 1846
McDONOUGH, Priscilla, wife of James and daughter of Samuel McCullough, died age 28.	MORE 27 June 1849
McELROY, Mrs. Catherine, died 23rd ult. near Warren, "respectable and estimable." (Probably widow of Warren who died in 1840.)	PWH 4 June 1846
McENNIS, Catherine in her 44th year and Joanna her sister in her 20th year, died in Baltimore in April.	MORE 28 May 1844
McEVOY, Margaret, consort of John, died yesterday age 29. Residence St. Charles St. Catholic cemetery.	SWERE 7 Feb 1848
McGIRK, Mrs. Elizabeth, consort of Andrew S, Esq., died 29 March in Lexington, Lafayette Co., in her 31st year. Left 3 children.	MORE 14 Apr 1834
McJILTON, Rachel, wife of James T., died 26 February age 30.	SWERE 28 Feb 1848
McKAY, Mrs. Sarah, died Monday 1st inst, wife of Harrison B. Esq. and daughter of Rev. Obadiah Jennings (decd) late of Nashville TN. Came to St. Louis about 2 years ago. Left 2 babies.	MORE 2 July 1844
McKEEN, Mrs. Ursule, relict of Hugh B., died 14th inst. Daughter of Joseph Barron; an early settler.	MODE 5 Aug 1846
McKELLY, Augusta age 16 died at the residence of Dr. George H. Schiers. (MORE says McKellops, died of typhoid, interred Presbyterian cem.	SWERE 26 Nov 1848
McKENNY, Mrs. Mary P., wife of J.H., died near Manchester 28 August.	MOAR 9 Sep 1836

McKINNEY, Mrs., wife of A.W., died in St. Charles Wednesday.	MORE 8 Aug 1834
McKNIGHT, Mrs. Fanny, wife of Thomas, died 5 December.	MORE 19 Dec 1825
McKNIGHT, Mrs. Zipporah, consort of William H., died	JASO 22 Dec 1838
McLEAN, Sarah of Ballston Springs died suddenly. Believed poisoned by her sister-in-law.	MORE 27 Feb 1846
McLEAN, Sarah committed suicide. (Laudanum) Resided on Spruce between Main and 2nd.	MORE 2 Nov 1844
McMILLEN, Mary, consort of John H. Esq., died Saturday 20th inst.	MORE 26 Apr 1844
McMURTRIE, Mrs. Alexander of Shelbyville died 10th inst of inflammation of the brain.	PWH 25 Mar 1847
MacMURTRY, Rosa Ann, daughter of Fanny and Levi, died in Williamsburg, Callaway Co. 13 August in her 12th year.	MORE 17 Aug 1848
McNAIR, Elvira, wife of A.R.; funeral from residence, Florida and Broadway.	MORE 22 Dec 1843
McNEES, Mrs. Elizabeth, relict of Samuel C., died at New Franklin in her 77th year on 7 June. Emigrated fr Rutherford Co TN to Old Franklin in 1816. Illness: tic douloureaux. Left children. Methodist.	BOLT 15 June? (1844-46)
McNEIL, Elizabeth, wife of Joseph of St. Louis, died in New York age 22. Funeral from residence of Rufus Keyser.	MORE 1 Aug 1846
McNULTY, Mary Ann, of Chariton Co., died 24 June ae 14. (Place not shown; she was traveling west.)	MORE 7 Oct 1850
McPHEETERS, Mrs., wife of Dr. William M., daughter of the late Maj. Cory Selden, died in Washington City. (SWERE 5 April gives her first name as "Pink."	MORE 31 Mar 1847
McPHEETERS, Mrs. Nancy B. died at the residence of her son 30 September in her 70th year.	PWH 8 Oct 1846
McPHERSON, Miss Emily died near St. Charles on the 10th inst. at the home of Howell (?Steen?)	MORE 23 Aug 1831
McPHERSON, Lydia Ann, wife of Isaac of St. Louis, died of congestive fever at Churchill, MO 2nd inst age 20.	MORE 16 Oct 1844
McQUIE, Miss Jane died 24 November on Noix Creek.	BGRAD 2 Dec 1843
McREE, McREA, Cornelia, daughter of Lt. Col. William, died 21st inst at the residence of Capt. Symington. (Name also shown as Caroline.)	MORE 28 May 1835 " 23 "
McVEIR, Ann, wife of George L., died in Baltimore 14 March. New Orleans pc.	MORE 11 Apr 1842

MACHATT, Mrs. Charles died in August at the home of her sister and brother-in-law, Lawson and Barbara Ann Lovering.   SOV 12 Sep 1834

MACKLIND, Ann died of cholera 29th inst age 58.   MORE 1 May 1849

MADDEN, Mrs. Catherine died 11th inst in her 44th year. Funeral from St. Patrick's Church.   MORE 12 Jan 1848

MAGRUDER, Mrs. Catherine Jane died at the residence of her brother Thomas Rose "Sunday last."   PWH 9 Apr 1842

MAGUIRE, Mrs. Mary Ann, consort of Michael, died at the residence of her father Joseph O'Neil yesterday.   MORE 24 Sep 1840

MAHAN, Mary, wife of James, died 30th ult. in her 45th year.   MIN 4 Sep 1824

MAHAN, Mrs. Sarah, consort of James, died age 59. Baptist since 1812. Hannibal and Palmyra pc.   COMB 27 Jan 1848

MAJOR, Mrs. died of cholera at Warsaw.   BRUNS 14 June 1849

MALLORY, Mrs. -- and child died of cholera at Waverly.   BRUNS 12 July 1849

MALONE, Mrs. Eliza, consort of Obadiah and daughter of John Johnson, died 31st inst in her 25th year. Left 5 small daughters.   INP 28 Aug 1824

MANARD, Mrs. Catherine, consort of Michael M., died 12 July in Texas.   MORE 17 Aug 1838

MANN, Mrs. Juliet W., consort of Alfred, died 7 July Saline Co. at Old Jefferson. Richmond Whig pc.   MORE 20 July 1839

MANN, Mary A., consort of J.E., died at Gallatin MO 21st inst age 33.   BRUNS 24 Feb 1849

MANNEY, Frances, wife of Jeremiah, died 13th inst. Funeral from Rev. Van Court's Church.   MORE 15 May 1849

MANSFIELD, Jane age 67 died 18 June at the crossing of the South Platte.
Elizabeth of Chariton Co. died 1 July at Ash Hollow. Left husband and children. Age 38.   MORE 7 Oct 1850

MARKELL, Sarah died 7th inst in Lincoln Co. age 80.   MOP 23 Aug 1846

MARKS, Ellen A., daughter of Dennis and Amira, died of inflammation of the lungs 14th inst in her 13th year. Resided on Collins St.   MORE 16 Jan 1847

MARSH, Sarah wife of Darius died "this morning."   SWERE 10 Jan 1848

MARSHALL, Isabella (or Arabella), wife of John Thorburn and daughter of Rev. A. Marshall, late of Edinburgh, decd., died, date not shown.   MORE 15 Jan 1840

MARSHALL, Mary Isabella, relict of James H., died 6th inst in her 21st year at the residence of her father, Capt. A. Harper, near Florissant. Louisville pc.   MORE 9 July 1845

MARTIEN, Nancy M., consort of Dr. James M. of Central Twp., died 22nd inst in her 29th year.	MORE 24 Oct 1846
MARTIN, Elizabeth Jane, wife of Elias B., died at Wellsburg, St. Charles Co., Saturday Sept. 18th in her 28th year. Late of Prince William Co., VA.	MORE 28 Sep 1841
MARTIN, Jane Catherine daughter of Robert, of Pike Co., died 30 July age 12.	SALT 7 Aug 1841
MARTIN, Mary E., only daughter of B.G. of Troy, died 23rd ult. at Ashley Female Seminary, age ca 15.	BGRAD 1 Jan 1842
MARTIN, Isabella P., daughter of J.P. and Sarah Ann, died in Morgan Co. MO age 11y 9m 20d. Formerly of Monroe Co. KY. Louisville *Journal* pc.	MORE 28 Apr 1847
MARVIN, Mrs. Mary E., daughter of Walker Louthan, died of consumption Friday.	PWH 22 July 1847
MASE, Nancy, wife of Walter, died near Frankford 20th inst age about 20.	BGRAD 30 Sep 1843
MASON, Jemima, widow of Henry, died 11 September.	MORE 17 Sep 1823
MASON, Miss Mahala died at the home of John H. Ferguson age about 45.	MORE 6 Jan 1842
MASSIE, Mrs. A.D., wife of Henry A., died at Boonville 21 June 1850.	MORE 27 June 1850
MASURE, Mrs. Marguerite H., daughter of Alexander Papin, died age 36. Interred Catholic cemetery.	MORE 19 Aug 1847
MATHEWS, Elizabeth C., wife of William, died 11 November in her 28th year. Funeral from residence of Mrs. Darst, Walnut between 3rd & 4th. Catholic cemetery.	MORE 12 Nov 1847
MATTHEWS, Manerva H., age about 14, died in Cape Girardeau.	JASO 20 Oct 1838
MATTHEWS, Mary E., wife of Stuart, died 10th inst ae 35.	MORE 14 May 1849
MATTINGLY, Helen Deretter died 13 April age 34.	SWERE 24 Apr 1848
MATTOX, Mildred A. died in St. Louis 18th inst in her 20th year. Consort of Edwin; originally from Richmond VA.	MORE 22 Dec 1836
MAUZEY, Mrs. Mary, of Saline Co., died at the residence of Gen. G. W. Lewis. Late of Harper's Ferry VA.	BRUNS 21 June 1849
MAWDELEY, Rebecca, wife of Richard Sr., died age 45. Residence on S. 5th St.	MORE 14 Dec 1847
MAXWELL, Louise Matilda, consort of Henry, daughter of William Warrance, late of Philadelphia. (Her infant son died 3 months later.)	MORE 2 Apr 1836
Caroline B., consort of Henry, died Saturday 7th inst in her 25th year.	MORE 9 Aug 1841

MEAD, Mrs. Susan, consort of Edward, died yesterday.   MORE 30 July 1839

MEECH, Eunice B. died 9th inst at the residence of her brother S. W.; daughter of Stephen Meech Esq. of Preston, Conn.   MORE 12 July 1837

MEGARY, Miss -- of St. Joseph. (no other data) (Notices of this date were reports of deaths of those emigrating westward.)   MORE 7 Oct 1850

MENNE, Caroline, wife of Henry, died Tuesday morning age 59.   SLDU 11 Sep 1846

MERRIMAN, Mrs. Enice died in St. Louis 11 April age 64. Formerly of Wallingford, Conn.   MORE 20 Apr 1839

MICHAUD, Miss Eleanore died Tuesday evening last of a lingering illness.   MORE 4 Sep 1818

MICHAU, Margaret, wife of the late St. Amant, died 2nd inst in Carondelet age 52.   MORE 5 May 1849

MILES, Emily Eleanor, wife of Edmond B., died 28th inst. Residence on St. Charles near 9th. Wheeling VA *Times* pc.   MORE 29 Dec 1846

MILLER, Gilly C., consort of Thomas, died 19th inst in her 30th year.   JEFRE 25 Feb 1837

MILLER, Lucinda, deceased; notice that her property is now in the hands of William Callaghan.   PWH 13 Nov 1844

MILLER, Prudence died 29 January at the residence of her son-in-law James K. White. In her 60th year. She emigrated from Shepherdstown VA in 1839.   PWH 3 Feb 1844

MILLER, Rachel died in Louisiana, MO age 18.   BGRAD 11 Mar 1843

MILLER, Mrs. Sarah died at the residence of William Dunn in this county 2nd inst.   BGRAD 8 June 1844

MILLER, Mrs. Sally died Friday last at the residence of her son-in-law N.J. Winston Esq. She was born in King & Queen Co. VA on 18 Aug. 1761. Married there, emigrated to KY, had one child born in KY in 1799. Came to MO in 1836. Had more than 100 descendants in KY, IL, and MO. A Baptist for more than 40 years.   JEM 30 Jan 1849

MILLER, Sarah died age 55. Funeral from residence of her son-in-law Archibald Carr Esq.   MORE 7 Jan 1846

MILLIGAN, Louisa wife of Edward died 27th inst in her 41st year. Resided Walnut between 7th-8th.   MORE 28 Jan 1847

MILLIGAN, MELLIGAN, Mrs. Margaret, daughter of James Timon, died 11th inst age 35.   MORE 12 Dec 1839

MILLINGTON, Mrs. Electa, consort of Ira, died 13th inst at the home of Dr. Seth Millington.   MORE 21 July 1829

MILLION, Rachel, consort of William, died Wednesday last in her 62nd year.   MODE 19 Aug 1846

47

MILLS, Mary, relict of the late John, formerly of Danville PA died 22 August in St. Ferdinand Twp. St. Louis Co.	SCOMB 28 Aug 1835
MILLS, Matilda, wife of A.L. Esq., died 16th inst age 49. Interred Presbyterian cemetery.	MORE 17 May 1849
MILLS, Patsy, daughter of James, died Wednesday last. (Her brother Micklebury Mills also died.)	BOLT 3 Oct 1840
MINARD, wife of Rev. Peter R. (Rector of St. Paul's Church. Funeral from the Church.	MORE 6 Oct 1840
MINKSON, Elizabeth Frances, wife of Addison C. and daughter of Lewis Castleman, died at Castleman's residence 7 December in her 23rd year. (Of Washington Co.)	MORE 1 Jan 1846
MINOR, Helen Augustine, daughter of Smith, Esq., late of Fairfax Co. VA died in her 18th year.	MORE 14 May 1849
Laura Ann, third daughter of Smith Esq., died 31 May near Flint Hills, St. Charles Co.	MORE 7 June 1849
MINOR, Mrs. Matilda, consort of Dr. T.J. of Florissant, died Monday morning after a lingering illness. Mother of 3 children, in her 25th year.	MORE 22 May 1834
MINOR, Sally C., wife of James L., died in Cole Co. 25th ult.	MORE 12 Aug 1845
MITCHELL, Alice H., wife of Dr. J.W.S., died 9 April in her 34th year.	MORE 10 Apr 1848
MITCHELL, Mrs., wife of Dr. Charles L., died 7 August. (Her husband died the previous day.)	MIN 26 Aug 1823
MITCHELL, Margaret Dillon, wife of John F., died "this morning" age 23.	MORE 1 July 1841
MITCHELL, Mrs. Helen H., died at her residence, corner Locust & 2nd, age 37. Native of Sandwich NH. Boston & NH pc.	MORE 7 Jan 1845
MITCHELL, Judith Ann, wife of A.S. and daughter of Henry J. Bodley, died 18th inst age 20.	MORE 20 June 1849
MITCHELL, Mrs. -- died 11th inst in Buffalo Twp. age about 50.	BGRAD 21 Sep 1844
MOBLOW, wife of John (St. Louis) came to St. Louis in May 1837 and died leaving a 5-day-old infant. Moblow left the infant with one Catherine Ditamin who advertises for him to get the child or make other arrangements.	MORE 20 Aug 1838
MOCK, Mrs. George died "Sunday" in Spencer Twp. age about 50. (Her husband died Wednesday age 55.)	BGRAD 31 Aug 1844
MOFFETT, Mrs. Charles, of Shelby Co., died 15th inst.	PWH 25 Sep 1841
MOLLOY, Albina, wife of John, died age 24. Resided 5th St. above Wash. Nashville pc	MORE 13 June 1849

MOLLOY, Sarah, wife of John, died 9th inst age 42.   MORE 10 Oct 1846
Funeral from residence 96 Washington Ave.

MONROE, Elizabeth, wife of Thomas and daughter of Abel   MIN 14 Apr 1826
Garrett of Saline Co., died 31 March.

MONTAGUE, Mrs. Jane S., consort of Thomas Esq., died   MORE 5 Jan 1846
at St. Charles 19th ult in her 38th year.
Richmond Whig pc.

MONTGOMERY, Mrs., wife of Rev., died at the missionary   STCHMO 3 Jan 1822
station near the Great Osage village on
27 October.

MOORE, Miss America, daughter of Alfred, died last   MORE 1 March 1831
evening; funeral this afternoon.

MOORE, Caroline L., wife of Capt. Henry J., died   MORE 29 June 1846
28th inst age 31.

MOORE, Mrs. Elizabeth, relict of John, died in   MORE 23 May 1842
Baltimore 10th inst in her 49th year.

MOORE, Elizabeth B., daughter of Maj. Robert, late   MORE 12 Jan 1836
of Ste. Genevieve, died at her brother's
residence in Lebanon, IL in her 19th year.

MOORE, Rebecca J., consort of William J. and daughter   BRUNS 19 July 1849
of Dr. John Bull, died 11th inst. (Her
second son, age 9, died at the same time.)

MOORE, Mrs. Ann, sister of Peter Lindell, died   MORE 15 July 1844
yesterday age 60. (Widow of Samuel?)

MOORE, Susan, consort of James R., died "this morning."   MORE 29 Sep 1843
Funeral from residence 14th N. of Franklin.

MORGAN Elizabeth, wife of Henry of St. Louis died
Wednesday 11 Sept.   MORE 13 Sep 1844

MORGAN Mrs. W.W., wife of Dr. J.G., died yesterday   MORE 4 Dec 1844
at the Planter's House. Recently of New York City.

MORGAN, Mary Stuart, consort of Franklin H., died   MORE 23 Jan 1847
22nd January age 36 y 1m. Resided 5th
between Locust and St. Charles.

MORRIS, Elizabeth, consort of James, died Friday   SWERE 10 Jan 1848
age 34.

MORRIS, Nancy, wife of Robert W., died Thursday.   MIN 29 Jan 1821

MORRISON, Mrs. Emilie, consort of Maj. James, died in   MORE 22 Aug 1834
St. Charles 20th inst. Many years a resident
of that place.

MORRISON, Clara S.M. daughter of Capt. P. died at   MORE 14 Mar 1846
Jefferson Barracks age 18y 3m 15d.

MORROW, Mrs. Lou Ann, consort of Christopher, late   BOLT 1 Apr 1843
of this county, died in Linn Co. 25th ult
in her 46th year.

MORTON, Eliza J., wife of William R., died at Lexington.   MIN 24 Aug 1833

MOSLEY, Phillis Ann wife of James died in Bowling Green Wednesday age about 18.	BGRAD 28 Sep 1844
MOSS, Mary W. wife of Dr. James W. died 21st inst at the residence of Col. O.P. Moss in her 64th year. "Wife and mother."	MORE 23 Jan 1843
MOSS, Mrs. Adeline, widow of Peter, died 20th inst near Spencerburg leaving 13 children. She was a Baptist. (Her husband's death notice also appeared on this date.)	BGRAD 11 Nov 1843
MOTHERSHEAD, Mrs. Elizabeth, consort of Charles of Jackson, died Tuesday last.	MOH 1 Apr 1820
MOXLEY, Mrs. Louisa died at the residence of her father William Scott 21 September, age 22, of consumption. Left 2 children.	BOLT 14 Oct 1843
Funeral notice for a Mrs. Moxley, sermon to be preached at Mt. Pleasant Monday after the 4th Lord's Day; may be the same person.	BOLT 17 Feb 1844
MULFORD, Lucinda, consort of Howell, formerly of Cincinnati, died 20 May.	SWERE 28 May 1849
MULLANPHY, Elizabeth, widow of John, died Sunday 16th inst.	MORE 17 Apr 1843
MULLIKIN, Mrs. Eliza, wife of Charles, died "last evening"	MORE 15 Jan 1841
MULLENS, Nancy, wife of William, died Sunday last. Left a large family of children.	MIN 5 Aug 1822
MUNROE, Mary Anne died 18th inst in her 34th year of a protracted illness. Formerly of Dinwiddie Co. VA.	MORE 30 Dec 1837
MUNSA, Martha, wife of William, died age 20y 7d. "Wife, mother."	MORE 19 June 1847
MURPHY, Amelia, wife of Joseph, died yesterday in her 38th year. (28th?)	NERA 4 Mar 1848
MURPHY, Mrs. Rachael, wife of David, died near Farmington 11 February.	MORE 23 Feb 1826
MURPHY, Miss Louisa died 3 October in her 22nd year.	INJN 10 Oct 1844
MURRAY, Eleanor died in Lillard Co. on 3 February. (Notice mentions her brothers Uriah and Reuben and twin daughters of Reuben.)	MIN 17 Apr 1824
MUSGROVE, Ann, consort of William and daughter of of decd Samuel Hudson died "last night."	LEXP 14 May 1845
MUSICK, Mrs. Lewis, drowned when a keelboat sank. (Her husband also drowned.)	MORE 4 May 1826
NABB, E.D., wife of C.W.; her parents, Dr. H. and Esther; and her only sister Ellen Fitzhugh all died in Baltimore in April.	SLDU 4 May 1847

NAPTON, Catherine T., sister of Judge W.B., died 22nd   MORE 4 July 1846
    inst. Age about 56, born in Saline Co., died   COMB 27 June 1846
    at L. F. Linn's.

NAYLOR, Jane, wife of John Esq., died at Dardenne   MORE 24 & 27
    Prairie, St. Charles Co., 17th inst in her   Feb 1835
    64th year.

NETHERLAND, wife of Col. Richard, died in Shelby Co.   PWH 25 Sep 1841
    15th inst.

NEWMAN, Dalila Elizabeth, daughter of Jacob of the   BORE 24 Oct 1843
    Boonville vicinity, died 21st inst in her
    16th year.

NEWMAN, Mary Jane Frances daughter of Michael and   SWERE 18 Oct 1847
    Margaret died 7 Oct. Jefferson City MO and
    Harrisonburg VA pc.   MORE 5 Feb 1849
    Julia A.H. eldest daughter of Michael and
    Margaret died 4th inst. Funeral from 4th St.
    Methodist Church.

NIFONG, Miss Meeke, died at the residence of her   MORE 31 Aug 1844
    father in Madison Co. MO 17th inst age 16.

NISBET, Mary Goode, wife of Robert and daughter of   MORE 8 Jan 1853
    John and Mary Lemoine of Petersburg VA died
    7th inst in her 25th year.

NOEL, Harriet, wife of Capt. Noel USA, died in St.   MORE 14 Mar 1838
    Louis Monday evening last. Left children.
    (Her son Nicholson Noel died that June.)

NORDMYRE, Elizabeth, wife of Charles, died in North   MODE 4 Dec 1848
    Glasgow Monday evening age 33.

NORRIS, Mary died 18th inst in her 58th year at the   MORE 20 Sep 1848
    residence of her son-in-law John Maguire on
    Bellefontaine Road. Funeral from the
    Cathedral to the Catholic cemetery.

NORRIS, Mrs. Mary W. died at her residence in   BOLT 26 July 1845
    Palestine MO in her 21st year. Consort of
    William W., daughter of Weeden Spenny,
    formerly of Fauquier, VA.

O'BANNON, Catherine, consort of Welton, died in her   INP 22 Dec 1821
    23rd year of ague and fever. Left
    "doating husband and fond relatives."
    (INP 9 March 1826 noted filing of estate of
    a Martha O'Bannon by Walton O'Bannon.)

O'BANNON, Mrs. Katharine Buger Boltom, wife of John Esq.   MORE 15 July 1844
    of Franklin Co., died 12th inst in her 51st year.
    Born Virginia, in Missouri many years.

O'CONNOR, Catherine, wife of Frederick, died 1 Oct.   PWH 9 Oct 1844
    in her 21st year.

O'FALLON, Mrs. Harriet, wife of Col. John, died last   MORE 16 Feb 1826
    Tuesday. (An obituary in MORE 23 Feb.)

O'FALLON, Mrs. Harriet, wife of Col. John, died last last Tuesday. (Long obituary on 23 Feb.)	MORE 16 Feb 1826
O'FLAHERTY, Catherine, wife of Thomas, died Saturday 27th in her 24th year.	MORE 30 Jan 1844
OLDHAM, Margaret, relict of William B., died at the residence of J. H. Kirby Saturday morning last.	PWH 31 Aug 1848
O'LEARY, Miss Ellen, formerly of Lynchburg VA, died in St. Louis 21st inst. "long troubled with an affliction of the lungs."	MORE 26 June 1834
OLIVER, Mrs. __, consort of William, died in Randolph Co. 9th inst.	BOLT 16 Apr 1842
OLMSTEAD, Esther died at the residence of her son-in-law Thomas Eustace 14th inst in her 87th year. Born in Ridgefield Conn., daughter of Jonathan Ingersoll.	MORE 15 Jan 1847
O'NEIL, Mary, relict of the late Hugh, died Saturday.	SWERE 14 May 1849
ORR, Mrs. Mary T., age 55, died 16 Feb. Funeral from residence of her son-in-law R. H. (or R.R.) Snow, corner 5th & Wash.	SWERE 19 Feb 1849
OURY, Mrs. Catherine, wife of Augustus, died Monday 8th inst.	SALT 13 June 1840
OVERLY, Hannah, wife of Henry, died at the residence of her son in Shamrock, Callaway Co., age 77 y 6m 14 d. Virginia pc.	BGRAD 20 Apr 1844
OVERTON, Mrs. Lewis died in Callaway Co.	PWH 27 Feb 1841
OWENS, Eliza, consort of Robert of St. Louis, died Friday 6th inst in Cape Girardeau.	MORE 12 Sep 1844
OWENS, Mrs. Fanny, consort of the late Samuel C. of Independence, died at the residence of her sister in Platte Co.	MODE 20 June 1848
OWINGS, Mary E., wife of Richard Esq. and eldest daughter of Richard L. Fant Esq. of Warren Co., died 6th inst age 3? (probably 33)	MORE 12 Sep 1848
PALMER, Betsy died at the residence of Col. David Bailey in Lincoln Co. in her 66th year.	MORE 29 Jan 1848
PAPIN, Caroline, daughter of Theodore Esq., died 1 Feb. in her 18th year.	MORE 2 Feb 1847
PAPIN, Mrs. Josephine, consort of Hypolite, died 24th inst at her residence 4 miles from St. Louis, age about 42. Funeral from Mr. Renard's to the Catholic cemetery.	MORE 25 Oct 1842
PAPIN, Sr. Joseph Marie died "yesterday morning at an advanced age."	MORE 19 Sep 1811
PAPIN, Marie Louise, consort of the late Joseph, died "Thursday last."	MORE 1 Mar 1817

PAPIN, Phoebe, wife of Joseph, died 18 May age 46.   MORE 20 May 1847
Funeral from residence on 2nd St. to the
Catholic cemetery.

PAPIN, Mme. Clementine, widow of Silvestre, died 26 Aug.   MORE 26 Aug 1839

PAPIN, Julia, consort of Alexander died yesterday in her   MORE 19 June 1844
56th year. Funeral from residence Main & Locust.
Catholic cemetery.

PARKER, Catherine, wife of Francis, died in Troy MO on   MORE 26 Mar 1833
on 12 March after a short but distressing
illness. Age 35.

PARKER, Mrs. John died age 60.   BGRAD 3 June 1843

PARROTT, Ann Virginia died 15 May age 17y 5m.   SWERE 17 May 1847

PARSONS, Elizabeth, wife of James, died 29 August in   MORE 13 Sep 1847
Gasconade Co. leaving four children. Formerly
of Hardy Co. VA.

PARSONS, Harriet R., wife of Dr., died in Miami (MO)   BRUNS 30 Aug 1849
2nd inst age about 38.

PARTUIT, Jeannette died at the home of her daughter,   MORE 17 Feb 1819
Widow Belland, on the ferry at the Missouri.
Widow of Etienne Lalande, a native of Detroit,
she was 114 years old.

PARVIN, Lydia Harris of Bloomington, IA died 20 May in   SWERE 28 May 1849
St. Louis at the residence of John P. Mulford.
(BRUNS 14 June says of Burlington IA, age 18,
daughter of John A.)

PATTERSON, Elizabeth, consort of G. W., died 13th inst   BRUNS 28 June 1849
in Saline Co. of a chronic liver complaint.
Age about 40, left 4 children.

PATTERSON, Mary William, daughter of Mrs. George Nevitt,   MORE 5 Jan 1837
died 29 December at the home of William Burd
in her 11th year.

PATTERSON, Sarah, consort of Edward, died 5th inst   SPAD 11 Oct 1845
age 48. Formerly of Tennessee. Left
6 children.

PATTEN, Mary B., sister of Nathaniel (late postmaster   MIN 9 Oct 1821
at Franklin) died age 19. Born in Roxbury MA,
also lived for a while in Montgomery Co. KY.

PATTEN, Matilda, wife of Nathaniel (editor of the Mo.   MIN 1 Jan 1830
Intelligencer) died in Fayette "last Sunday."

PAUL, Mrs. Louise, wife of Gabriel, died Tuesday night.   MORE 30 Oct 1832

PAUL, Eulalie, consort of Rene, died on a voyage to New   MORE 14 Apr 1835
Orleans. (SCOMB 18 May says that the boat was the
Michigan and she died near Vicksburg. She was
returned for burial in the Catholic cemetery.)

PAYNE, Mrs. Lucy T., consort of James R., died 2 April   COMB 13 Apr 1848
age 27y 2m. Left children. Richmond Whig pc.

PAYNE, Maria M., daughter of George, died 3rd inst from the effects of a fall from a horse. Near Glasgow. (Obituary from Monticello Seminary.) — BOLT 13 May 1843

PEACHER, Mrs. Alexander, of Howard Co., committed suicide while deranged. — MORE 17 Mar 1848

PEASE, Athalie, consort of Joseph B., died yesterday in her 29th year. Resided on S. 4th St. Interred Catholic cemetery. — MORE 5 Oct 1848

PEEBELS, Miss Jane died at Franklin 1st inst. — MIN 12 Oct 1826

PENCE, Mrs. Elizabeth, consort of Adam, died (date not shown). Was a Baptist. — FAR 22 Sep 1836

PENNELL, Elizabeth, consort of William D., died at the the residence of her father Caton Usher Esq., in Chariton Co. (MO) age 16y 9m 13d. — MORE 10 Mar 1843

PENNEY, Martha, wife of Isaac, died 16th inst. Resided Walnut St. Between 5th & 6th. — MORE 17 Feb 1849

PENRICE, Mrs. Julia R., wife of John B. of Princeton MA and oldest daughter of Mrs. A. R. Corbin of St. Louis died 25 February in her 22nd year. Interred Methodist burying ground. — MORE 8 Mar 1841

PERRY, Mrs. Frances T. died 4 September age 57 while visiting her children. Originally from the vicinity of the University of Virginia. Home, MountBelle, site not given. — MORE 6 Sep 1837

PERRY, Julia A., consort of John D. died 28 June near Glasgow. — BRUNS 5 July 1849

PERRY, Lucy, consort of Nathan, died at Montreal in her 38th year on 26 October. — MORE 17 Feb 1844

PERRY, Sarah H., wife of Prof. Thomas H., died 27 June age 38. Philadelphia and Boston pc. — SWERE 3 July 1848

PETTIBONE, Louisa A., wife of the late Rufus, died in Louisiana MO 6 October age 31. — MORE 18 Oct 1827

PETTIBONE, Mrs. Martha, consort of Levi of Bowling Green, died at the residence of Edwin Draper in Louisiana MO age 46. Erie PA pc.
(BGDB says Draper was her son-in-law and gives date of death as 15 April.) — MORE 18 Apr 1845

PETTIT, Maria E. died 25 March in Chicot Co. AR. — MORE 12 June 1841

PEYTON, Ann Elizabeth, daughter of John and Elizabeth, died 6th inst age 13. — FULT 24 Aug 1849

PEYTON, Miss Ellen died in Boonville 8th inst after a lingering illness. — COMB 11 Mar 1847

PHILLIPS, Adaline, daughter of Dr. G. W., died 26 June age 18y 9m. Late of Ithaca NY. — MORE 29 June 1840

PHILLIPS, Mary, consort of Joseph M., died Sunday evening last in Union Twp. — PWH 15 Jan 1845

PHILLIPS, Polly, consort of James, died 23 July in her 63rd year. MODE 8 Aug 1848

PHILLIPS, Mrs. Sarah died 16th inst. PWH 17 Sep 1845

PHILIPSON, Susanna, wife of Simon, died in St. Louis on 1 October. Late of Philadelphia. SLINQ 20 Oct 1821

PICKETT, Mrs. Sarah Jane died of cholera in Palmyra. MORE 28 June 1833

PIGGOTT, Emilia Ann, Sister of Charity, native of Ireland, died 9th inst age about 45. SOV 27 Sep 1833

PIGOTT, Catherine, wife of John, died in Lexington MO 21st ult in her 22nd year. Late of St. Louis. (Her only child, John, died 17 May age 5 m.) MORE 4 June 1849

PILCHER, Mrs. Joshua died Monday 3rd inst. Interred in Episcopal cemetery. MORE 7 June 1843

PINNELL, Adelia, daughter of F. A. and Sarah, died in Clinton 8th inst age 12y 10m. BORE 19 July 1845

PITKINGTON, Alice, wife of H., died 23rd inst. MORE 25 Jan 1849

PITTS, Sarah Catherine, wife of Richard, died in St. Louis County 6 July. MORE 9 July 1841

PLACIDE, Jane "of the Theatre" died 19th inst in New Orleans. (SCOMB says of the "Camp Street Theatre." MORE 30 May 1835

POCOCKE, Mrs. Charlotte, consort of William H., died "last evening." Funeral 4 pm today. MORE 9 June 1829

POINTER, Caroline Eliza, wife of the late John L., died at the residence of her father near Plaquemines LA 19 May. (Obituary of John L. 9 Jan 1844 says that he had 2 children.) MORE 1 June 1844

PORTER, Catharine Isabella, daughter of William H., died age 14y 6m. BRUNS 29 July 1848

PORTER, Mrs. Mary, died 4th inst in her 64th year. "Raised 10 children." COMB 14 Jan 1847

POTTER, Mrs. Hannah, consort of the late Capt. Robert, formerly of Bowdoin, Maine, died yesterday of a bilious complaint, age 55 years. Funeral from the residence of James C. Cummins to the Catholic burying ground. MORE 22 Aug 1821

POTTS, Mrs. Mary, consort of John, died in Boonville yesterday. BOLT 14 Aug 1841

POWERS, Mary Matilda, daughter of John G., died yesterday age 19. Funeral from residence on Olive St. between 8th & 9th. MORE 29 Jan 1842

POYNTER, Margaret M., wife of Dr. James E., died in Warsaw, MO 25th inst. Daughter of F. H. Watkins Esq. of Callaway Co. MORE 4 Dec 1848

PRENTIS, Harriette, wife of Russell E., died 25th inst. Funeral from First Presbyterian Church. MORE 27 Nov 1848

PRESTON, Mary Landonia, eldest daughter of William R. and Eliza, died suddenly at Preston Hall in St. Charles County. Richmond Whig pc. — MORE 25 Aug 1837

PRICE, Mary Ann, consort of George B., publisher of the Salt River Journal, died (date not given). "Three babies." Methodist. — SALT 1 Aug 1840

PRICE, Patience, wife of John R., died suddenly 26th ult at Bruncwick. — BOLT 7 June 1845

PRICE, Phoebe, consort of Jeremiah, died yesterday. — MORE 20 June 1835

PRICE, Mrs. Mary, consort of Risdon H., died 24th inst in St. Ferdinand. Interred Bissell family burying ground. — MORE 25 Jan 1845

PRIEST, Sarah T. died 30 September in Shelbyville; her sister Elizabeth died 1 October. Late of Warren County VA. — PWH 5 Nov 1842

PRIMM, Mrs. Amelia, wife of Wilson, died yesterday in her 25th year. Funeral from residence to the Catholic cemetery. — MORE 6 May 1841

PRINCE, Mary Jane, wife of Dr. David, died 24th inst in her 33rd year. Resided #170 11th St. Jacksonville, Quincy, Cincinnati pc. — MORE 26 Jan 1849

PRINGLE, Mrs. Sally, wife of Norman Esq., died at Hickory Grove, Montgomery Co., in her 50th year. — MORE 4 Dec 1832

PRITCHETT, Mrs. Mary, consort of Jesse, died Monday last age 24. — MORE 2 June 1841

PRITCHETT, Mrs. ___ died of cholera in Palmyra. — MORE 28 June 1833

PRYOR, Mrs. ___, wife of Anthony, died Thursday last. — MORE 21 Nov 1840

PTOMEY, Rachel D. C., wife of Robert, died "last evening" in her 21st year. — PWH 18 Feb 1843

PUGH, Mariam, wife of Washington A., died "Friday week" age 19 or 20. Methodist. — BRUNS 21 Apr 1849

PULLIAM, Lucy Ann, daughter of William, died 15th inst of pneumonia age about 17. — PWH 20 Jan 1848

PURCELL, Mrs. Eliza Ann died 21st inst. Funeral from St. John's Church to Episcopal cemetery. — MORE 22 Feb 1849

PURDEN, Maria, consort of Alexander and daughter of H. T. Brown of Linn, died of puerperal fever, aged about 19. Left 2 small children. — BRUNS 31 May 1849

PURDOM, Mrs., wife of W. T. of New London, Ralls Co., drowned herself in Salt River lately. (MORE on 1 Dec. gives her name as Frances and states that she had been despondent since the death of her husband. — BRUNS 2 Dec 1848

PURSE, Mrs. Elizabeth, wife of Samuel H., died 25th ult at Ashley. Left an infant. — SALT 1 May 1841

PYE, Emily B., wife of Jonas R., died 3 March age 21.   MORE 5 Mar 1845

QUARLES, Martha E. died in St. Louis yesterday morning   MORE 10 Aug 1838
    in her 19th year.

QUICK, Mrs. Francis, wife of Daniel of St. Louis Co.,   MORE 12 Feb 1842
    died 2 February.

QUIRK, Mary, daughter of Mary Riley, died 13th inst age   MORE 14 May 1849
    22 years. Funeral from residence, 56 Elm, to
            Catholic cemetery.

QUISENBERRY, Catherine, consort of William, died in Osage JINQ 7 Nov 1843
    County age 27. Formerly of Virginia. Left
    2 children. Died 16 October.

RAILEY, George Ellen, only child of George and Maria,   PWH 9 Nov 1848
    died of scarlet fever 26th inst in her 17th year.

RAINES, Mrs. Jane H. died 1st inst in Lewis Co. in her   PWH 19 July 1849
            55th year.

RAMSAY, Mrs. Robert was killed on "Saturday last"   MORE 27 May 1815
    two miles from the old Charrette settlement
    in St. Charles Co. (Indians? Ramsay and their
    three children were also killed.)

RANDALL, Mrs. Cynthia died 12 July age 49y 2m 1d. Sister   BGRAD 20 July 1844
    of Jesse R. Smith of Ashley, formerly of
    Bowling Green KY.

RANDOLPH, Sarah E., wife of B. H. Esq., died 23rd inst   MORE 25 Mar 1848
    age 28. Resided #184 Olive St.

RANKIN, Sarah, consort of C.S., died in Herculaneum   MORE 6 Mar 1846
    1 March age 22.

RANSOM, Lydia T., wife of Duke, died yesterday age 38.   MORE 18 June 1842
    Funeral from residence on Second St., 4
    doors below Poplar St.

RANSON, Elizabeth, wife of Ambrose, died in Union,   MORE 2 June 1843.
    Franklin Co., 24th ult. Late of Buckingham
    Co. VA. Age 38.

RAYBURN, Mary, wife of Col. S. S., died Friday evening   MORE 19 Feb 1842
    in her 33rd year. Funeral from residence on
            Broadway.

READING, Mrs. Nancy died at Grassey Creek 20th inst   BGRAD 22 Oct 1842
            age 72.

READING, Nancy G., wife of Joseph of Pike Co., died   BGRAD 30 Apr 1842
    22nd inst in her 43rd year.

REAGEN, Mrs. --, wife of Reizen, killed by Indians   MORE 16 July 1814
    with her small son and daughter near Wood
    River, Illinois Territory -- Mr. Reagen
    sends notice to friends in Kentucky and
            Tennessee.

REDFIELD, Charlotta, consort of Capt. E., died at St. Ferdinand Twp. 1st inst age 27.	MORE 9 Dec 1840
REID, Jennet, wife of David, died 5th inst. Funeral from residence 4th between Locust & Vine. (Her husband, a native of Scotland, died 23 April age 67 -- SWERE 30 April)	MORE 6 June 1849
REED, Chloe, widow of Jacob, died Friday last.	MORE 28 Aug 1822
REED, Julia A. died 9 May. Daughter of the late Capt. Jacob, an early resident, and sister of Mrs. Asa Wilgus of St. Louis.	SWERE 14 May 1849
REEL, Harriet, consort of John W. Esq., died in Louisville Wednesday 19th inst.	MORE 28 June 1833
REEVES, Martha, consort of William, age 18, died 14 November at the home of her father, Major James Brown.	MIN 20 Nov 1829
REEVES, Patsy, wife of Col. Benjamin H., died last Saturday at Fayette.	MIN 16 May 1835
REGAN, Mrs. --, wife of John, died 13 June in her 36th year. Resided Chestnut St. between 3rd & 4th. Pittsburgh & New York pc.	MORE 15 June 1847
REID, Charlotte Ann, wife of Hugh T. Esq., died 8th inst at Ft. Madison, Iowa Territory.	MORE 23 July 1842
REID, Mrs. Sarah Ellis, consort of Christopher C. and daughter of Shelton Rutherford, died in her 25th year near Middle Grove, in Monroe Co., 10th inst. Paris Mercury pc.	BOLT 16 Aug 1845
REILLY, Mary Ann, relict of the late Michael, died Monday last.	MORE 2 June 1836
RELFE, Mrs. Jane died at the residence of her son the Hon. James H. in Caledonia 17th inst. Wheeling VA pc.	MORE 23 Sep 1844
REYNOLDS, Mrs. Elizabeth, age 57, died at the residence of her son Wesley Hieronimous of this county. Methodist many years.	BOLT 29 Aug 1840
REYNOLDS, Eliza Ann, consort of Jesse D., died 30 April of pulmonary consumption leaving 5 infant children.	PWH 6 May 1847
RHODES, Maria H., wife of E. H., died (date not shown). Formerly of Fauquier VA.	BGRAD 27 July 1844
RICE, Mary, consort of John, died Christmas day in her 35th year.	MORE 26 Dec 1848
RICHARDS, Mrs. died "last Saturday at an advanced age." (Probably Jane whose estate record is shown later.)	MORE 21 Nov 1825
RIDDLE, Mrs. Abigail died 4th inst age 85.	MORE 5 Mar 1849
RIDDLE, Jane, Esther (age 24) and __ age 18 all died in June at the Crossing of the South Platte. (All of Pike Co.)	MORE 7 Oct 1850

RIDDELE, Sarah, consort of Col. Alexander, died   MORE 7 June 1844
       yesterday. Funeral from residence, Walnut
       St. between 6th & 7th. (Her infant son died
       6 weeks later age 4 months.)

RIDDLESBARGER, Hazelet, died 15th inst in her 16th year. BOLT 19 Oct 1844

RIDGELY, Frances, wife of F. L., died 28th inst.   MORE 30 Sep 1846

RIDGELY, Ann Rebecca, consort of Dr. R. G., died   MORE 15 July 1828
                          yesterday.

RIDGELY, Mrs. Jane Olivia, consort of Nicholas H. Esq., MORE 9 Aug 1833
       died of cholera Tuesday evening last. Left
       family in Maryland.

RIFFE, Mrs. Mary, wife of John Esq., died in Ray Co.   LEXP 14 July 1844
       Friday 12th inst in her 52nd year.

RIGGS, Fanny Behn, wife of Lawrison and daughter of   SWERE 8 Jan 1849
       Benjamin Clapp Esq., died 4 January.

RIGGS, Mrs. Sophia Theresa, wife of Lawrence and   MORE 10 Jan 1841
       daughter of Joseph Crittenden, late of
       Georgetown DC, died 6th inst.

RILEY, Elizabeth died 28th ult in her 26th year.   MORE 18 Oct 1845
       Late of Baltimore and Richmond VA.

RILEY, Mrs. --, of 3th St. below Convent, died when   MORE 25 Apr 1845
       she was thrown off a porch in a quarrel with
       Martin Walters. (He was examined and dismissed.)

RILEY, Mary age 18y 6m died 14 November.   SWERE 19 Nov 1848

RIPLEY, Mrs. -- died at Gravois "a few days ago."   MORE 19 Oct 1816

RIPLEY, Mrs. Esther W., wife of Jacob, died   MORE 23 Aug 1827
                          "last Tuesday."

RIPPEY, Mrs. Violina P., consort of Matthew, died   MORE 23 Feb 1844
       Wednesday age 35. (additional note on 27 March
       gives name is Vilinia and notes that she was
       formerly of Monroe Co. VA.)

RISKE, Mrs. Charlotte C.L., died at the residence of her MIN 21 May 1821
       son Major James C. Ludlow of Franklin Saturday
       last in her 52nd year. (MIN 28 August adds that
       she was the daughter of Gen. James Chambers,
       wife of Israel Riske.)

ROBERTS, _ "a lady" from Howard County en route to   BOLT 10 June 1843
       Osceola died at the residence of Silas W.
       Logan, Richland Twp., Morgan Co., about 20 May.
       She was traveling with a man named Meredy, had
       an 8-month-old infant, and was the daughter of
       Wade Whitney, formerly of Howard. Friends are
       requested to come and get the child.

ROBARDS, Mary S., daughter of William and Dorcas,   COP 2 Dec 1842
       died 22 November in her 23rd year.

ROBERTS, Miss Perlina age 16 died 19 April in Boone Co. MIN 27 Apr 1833

ROBERT, Sarah, wife of Sanderson, died 29th ult at the residence of D. Hough. Lately of New Orleans, formerly of Philadelphia.   MORE 3 Feb 1845

ROBERTS, Mrs. Elizabeth, wife of William F. Esq., died in Potosi 12th inst in her 53rd year. Half-sister to the present governor of Illinois. "Wife, mother." Presbyterian. Interred Potosi cemetery.   MORE 20 Dec 1842

ROBERTSON, Mrs. Sarah died Saturday last in Lexington of consumption.   LEXP 14 May 1845

ROBINSON, Deborah Arnett, consort of Gordon, died 19 June aboard the steamboat Timoleon. Many years resident of St. Louis. (SWERE of same date gives middle name as Annette.)   MORE 3 July 1848

ROBINSON, Mrs. Jane Amanda, relict of the Rev. Charles S., died at the home of her son-in-law Thomas Lindsey Esq. near St. Charles.   MORE 3 Sep 1833

ROBERTSON, Sarah Ann Lambert, wife of Thomas B. and youngest daughter of Robert Lambert of Garstang, Lancashire died age 21.   SLDU 5 Sep 1846

ROBINSON, Sarah Eulalie, wife of A. S. Esq. and daughter of P. Provenchere died in her 22nd year.   MORE 28 Aug 1840

ROBINSON, Mrs. Sophia, wife of M., died 1st inst in her 62nd year. Resided Hazel & 2nd St.   MORE 2 Dec 1848

ROBNETT, Mary, wife of Samuel and daughter of William Ritchie, Esq. died Thursday last.   PWH 3 Aug 1848

ROCHEBLAVE, Mrs. Susan, wife of Philip, died 14 Feb.   MORE 23 Feb 1824

ROCK, Mary Ann, wife of A. C. and daughter of James Herndon, died near Carrollton Monday last.   BRUNS 16 Mar 1848

ROGERS, Mrs. Eliza J., consort of Leonard J., died near Bowling Green. Methodist.   SALT 22 May 1841

ROGERS, Mrs. Sarah died 9th inst in Warren Twp. in her 85th year.   PWH 20 Apr 1848

ROGERSON, Maria, consort of David of New Orleans, died 7th inst. New Orleans Picayune pc.   MORE 9 June 1845

ROQUES, Margaret, wife of John, died 11 Nov. Funeral at their farm near Carondelet.   MORE 13 Nov 1847

ROSE, Mrs. Ellen, consort of E. H., died 11th inst at Florissant.   MORE 22 Mar 1838

ROSE, Mrs. Sarah, wife of Joseph, died 2 February in her 25th year. Member of Christian Church.   SPAD 6 Feb 1847

ROSS, Charlotte, consort of Thomas, died 11th inst. (see also Routt)   PWH 15 Apr 1843

ROUND, Mrs. Henrietta, died (date not shown). Funeral from residence of her niece Mrs. Turpin on Sixth St.   MORE 21 Oct 1842

ROUTT, Mrs. Ann Maria, wife of Elbert and daughter of Thomas Ross, died in Lewis Co. 5th inst. Maysville KY pc. — PWH 7 June 1849

ROUTIN, Mme. Michel died Monday 27 November. — MORE 28 Nov 1837

ROWE, Rosina, wife of James S., manager of the American Theatre, died the Saturday before 18 May. (MORE 30 May gives date as 19 May and place of death as New Orleans.) — SCOMB 29 May 1835

RUCKER, Mrs. Flora, wife of Lieut. Rucker and daughter of Joseph Cooley of the Cherokee nation and niece of John Ross, principal chief of the Cherokee Nation, died at Ft. Gibson 27 June. — MORE 19 July 1845

RUCKER, Martha, daughter of Elizabeth, recently of Lynchburgh VA, died in St. Louis 21st ult. — MORE 24 Nov 1836

RULAND, Ann F., wife of General John D., died yesterday in her 46th year. Presbyterian cemetery. — MORE 25 June 1845

RULAND, Keziah, consort of Israel, died in Troy, MO 11th inst age 48. Formerly of Washington Co. PA. "Parent." — MORE 16 July 1841

RUSH, Mrs. Margaret died 30 May in her 52nd year. — PWH 18 June 1845

RUSSELL, Miss Abigail M. died in Boone Co. 14th inst. Daughter of the late Robert S. and Deborah, in her 61st year. — FULT 5 Oct 1849

RUSSELL, Deborah, widow of Gn. Robert S., died at the home of her son-in-law Jefferson Garth Esq. in the vicinity of Columbia on 11 June, age 76. — COP 25 June 1842

RUSSELL, Mrs. Elizabeth Ann, consort of James Esq., proprietor of this newspaper, died in her 34th year after a lingering illness. Left 2 children. — INP 2? Sep 1823

RUTTER, Matilda, wife of John P. Esq., died 28 March. — PWH 30 Mar 1848

SACKETT, Mrs. Lucy Ann, consort of William H., died in St. Charles Co. 24 November in her 24th year. Late of Frederick Co. VA. (LUCKETT?) — MORE 29 Nov 1837

SAFFARRANS, Mrs. Mary, wife of George, died Wednesday last in her 65th year. Left 12 children. — MODE 28 Mar 1848

SALISBURY, Mrs. Eliza Irene, consort of Philander, died 30 September age 29y 8m. Funeral from residence 2½ miles from St. Louis on Bellefontaine Road. — MORE 2 Oct 1841

SALISBURY, Harriet, of St. Charles, died yesterday. Funeral from Unitarian Church, 4th & Pine. — MORE 27 Sep 1843

SAMUEL, Mrs. Catherine, wife of Jamison Esq., died at Hannibal 8th inst. — MORE 12 June 1843

SAMUEL, Elizabeth, wife of Edward M., died in Clay Co. 17 May age 37. — BRUNS 31 May 1849

SANDERS, wife of Dr. R. H. died at Glasgow.	BRUNS 26 July 1849
SANDERSON, Eliza, wife of Uriah, died 27 June. Louisville KY pc.	SWERE 28 June 1847
SANDFORD, Elizabeth, consort of T. S. Esq. and daughter of John Hutcherson died 24th ult in her 24th year. Member of the Christian Church at Houston.	PWH 1 Jan 1846
SANFORD, Emilie C., consort of J.F.A. and daughter of P. Chouteau Jr. died aboard the George Collier from New Orleans Monday last.	MORE 28 Apr 1836
SANGUINETTE, Cecelia, wife of Charles Sr., died in her 56th year. Funeral from St. Xavier Church.	MORE 6 June 1849
SANSBURY, Nancy, daughter of Reason, died Thursday in her 19th year of the "prevailing summer disease"	JEFRE 15 Aug 1840
SAPPINGTON, Mrs. Jemima, consort of John, died 27th ult at the Gravois in her 54th year. She "leaves 16 children to lament her loss."	MORE 8 Oct 1814
SARPY, Pelagie Labadie Gregoire died Wednesday last age 58.	MORE 26 Apr 1833
SARPY, Mrs. Jane Adele, wife of John H. (No date)	MORE 3 Apr 1832
SARADA, SARRADE, Rosalie died 12 November at the residence of her son-in-law Amadee Valle Esq. age 64.	MORE 15 Nov 1837
SAUCIER, Frances, wife of the late Judge, died 18th at the residence of her son in Portage des Sioux, in her 83rd year. She was born in Kaskaskia in 1757.	MORE 25 Feb 1840
SAUCIER, Mrs. Catherine, died 26 February at Portage des Sioux, age 78. Last of the original settlers of that village and half-a-century neighbor to Mrs. Marianne Clairmont who died a few hours earlier. They were buried in the same grave.	MORE 3 Mar 1845
SAUNDERS, Mrs. Mary, wife of Christopher, died yesterday morning. Formerly of Hartford, CT.	MORE 28 Aug 1832
SAUNDERS, Mrs. Martha died suddenly at the residence of William D. Swinney in Howard Co., 4th inst, in her 67th year. Methodist. Louisville pc.	BOLT 11 June 1842
SAUSSER, Mary died 6th inst in her 59th year. Funeral from the residence of her son John Riggin.	MORE 7 Dec 1841
SAVAGE, Mrs. Adelaide, wife of William H., a merchant of St. Louis, died lately in Barnstable MA.	MORE 19 Apr 1827
SAVAGE, Mrs. Hope, consort of Dr. Samuel, died 22 Dec. at Barnstable MA age 75.	MORE 18 Jan 1831

SAVAGE, Mrs. Mary Jane, consort of Rev. F. A., died　　BOLT 30 Aug 1845
　　at Milwaukee, Wisconsin Territory, 8th inst.
　　Formerly of Campbell Co. VA.

SCHINOTTI, Mrs. Lucy, wife of J. F., a painter, died　　MORE 10 Jan 1844
　　8th inst at St. Louis Hospital.

SCHROEDER, Hannah Carter, wife of Charles H. Esq. and　　MORE 12 Mar 1846
　　daughter of Henry H. of Philadelphia, died
　　10th inst in her 46th year. Resided 4th &
　　Spruce. Philadelphia pc.

SCHROEDER, Henrietta Virginia, wife of the Rev. W. H.　　MORE 3 Sep 1850
　　of Clinton, Henry Co., died 11 August.
　　Late of Richmond VA.

SCHROTER, Agnes, wife of George, died at West Ely　　PWH 24 Sep 1846
　　16th inst in her 21st year.

SCOTT, Miss Alzira Virginia died 25 December 1846 at　　SWERE 18 Jan 1847
　　the home of her father, William Scott Esq., in
　　Howard Co. (MODE 11 Jan gives date as 30 Dec.)
　　Age 21.

SCOTT, Eliza, wife of Andrew, died in Pope Co.,　　MORE 7 Apr 1835
　　Arkansas Territory, age about 40.

SCOTT, Catherine, consort of John Esq. of Ste.　　MORE 13 Jan 1816
　　Genevieve, died Tuesday evening, 24th ult.

SCOTT, Julia, consort of E., died 12th inst in her　　BRUNS 17 Feb 1848
　　22nd year.

SCOTT, Mary, wife of William C., died 23rd inst ae 32.　　MORE 24 Apr 1849
　　Funeral from Scott's Hotel.

SCOTT, Mary S., wife of Reuben, died 7 July age 49.　　FULT 4 Aug 1848
　　A native of Tennessee, then moved to Kentucky;
　　charter member of Auxvasse Church. Left "family."

SCOTT, Mrs. -- of Cape Girardeau died at Ft. Laramie　　MORE 7 Oct 1850
　　on 26 June.

SEARS, Mrs. Elizabeth, consort of Joseph of this　　BOLT 2 Oct 1841
　　vicinity, died 26 September. (BOLT 5 Mar 1842
　　notes funeral to be preached for wife of Joseph
　　Sears on the 2nd Sunday in March, College Church.)

SEAT, Mrs. Elizabeth died 21 August in her 25th year.　　WEM 5 Sep 1839
　　Left husband and 4 children.

SEBREE, Maria, daughter of Major Ural, died 26th ult　　BRUNS 16 Dec 1848
　　in Howard Co. age 18.

SELKIRK, Mrs. Lydia, consort of Alexander, died 6th　　MORE 8 Jan 1844
　　inst age 38.

SELKIRK, Harriet Ann, wife of Alexander, died Monday　　MORE 29 July 1845
　　28th inst. Funeral from residence, 2nd St.
　　between Plum and Poplar.

SELLERS, Mrs. Amanda M. F., wife of Capt. Isaiah, died　　MORE 12 Dec 1843
　　10th inst age 27.

SENTER, Catherine, daughter of Dr. Stephen and Margaret,   FREEP 22 Aug 1833
    died 10th inst of bilious fever. Methodist.

SHACKELFORD, Mrs. Anne, consort of R. D., died in her   BORE 9 Apr 1843
    37th year, leaving a large family of children.

SHACKFORD, Charlotte Louisa, consort of Charles C.,   MORE 21 Oct 1845
    died at Burlington IA 13th inst age 25.

SHANNON, Mrs. Anne, relict of John, died at the residence
    of her brother in Lincoln County 30th ult.   MORE 21 Dec 1839
    Formerly of Shelby Co. KY.

SHANNON, Mrs. George died Tuesday 12th inst in her 40th   MORE 20 Sep 1833
    year leaving husband and children. Death due
    to typhus after a long illness. Husband U. S.
    Attorney for Missouri.

SHANNON, Alcey Jane, wife of John F. (or H.) died Thuesday   PWH 13 Aug 1845
    night last. (Her daughter Elizabeth Amelia
    died a few days later in her 9th year.)

SHANNON, Sarah D., consort of John H., died 27th ult.   PWH 2 Aug 1849

SHANNON, Mrs. Sydney died at the residence of her   MORE 16 Sep 1847
    grandson C. E. Loring in her 86th year. One
    of the first settlers of Kentucky. A
    Presbyterian for 50 years.

SHARP, Mrs. Harriet, consort of Jacob L., died 10th inst   MORE 21 June 1842
    of measles at Danville, Montgomery Co., in her
    46th year. Left 4 children.

SHATTUCK, Miss Hannah E. died 2nd inst in St. Louis,   MORE 7 June 1839
    age 17. Formerly of N. Reading MA.

SHAW, Mrs. Elizabeth, consort of John, died 9th   SALT 24 July 1841
    inst in her 27th year. (Her daughter Elizabeth
    died a short time later age 7 days.)

SHAW, Miss Elizabeth died 5th inst age about 19.   MIN 11 Nov 1820

SHAW, Mrs. Mary, consort of Thomas H. of Commerce,   MORE 17 July 1844
    Scott County, died there 14th inst. "Mother,
    wife."

SHAWK, Mrs. Mary Ann, wife of Samuel, died yesterday   MORE 26 July 1843
    age 23. Funeral from residence, St. Charles St.

SHEPHERD, Mrs. Mary -- funeral to be preached at the   SALT 4 July 1840
    home of Jesse Shepherd, 3rd Sabbath of July,
    by Rev. Fuqua.

SHIELDS, Mrs. Nancy died in this county 9th inst in   BOLT 23 Nov 1844
    her 74th year.

SHOBE, Mrs., wife of Abraham, died 11th inst at   MORE 13 Mar 1835
    Darst Bottom.

SHREVE, Mary, wife of Capt. Henry, died in her 55th   MORE 27 Feb 1846
    year. "Wife, mother, grandmother."

SHRYER, Mrs. Gertrude died yesterday in St. Louis of   MORE 29 Aug 1840
    consumption. Resided 6th & Green.

SIBLEY, Harriet Carney, consort of L. T. Esq., died at Detroit. (SCOMB 29 May 1835 says Harriet Larned, wife of Lieut E. S., USA, gives date of death as 26 May.)   MORE 28 May 1835

SIEMAN, Mrs __, killed by a McDaniel slave near Washington, Franklin Co. Her 7-year-old son was injured.   MORE 15 Mar 1847

SIMMONS, Mrs. Elizabeth, consort of the Late Dr., died 7th inst at the residence of the Hon. John C. Edwards in Jefferson City.   JEFRE 9 Sep 1843

SIMMONS, Jane, consort of Dr. R. P., died in her 38th year. Native of Carlisle PA, later of Cincinnati.   MORE 26 Nov 1838

SIMMONS, Eliza M., consort of Dr. R. P., died 4th inst age 41y 1m 3d. Funeral from residence on Eighth Avenue.   MORE 8 Mar 1848

SIMPSON, Elizabeth, wife of Martin of St. Louis.   MORE 9 July 1833

SIMPSON, Sarah Jane, daughter of James W. and granddaughter of Erasmus, died 19th inst in St. Charles County. (Her grandfather died at the same time and place.)   MORE 24 Sep 1840

SINGLETON, Mrs. Mary Ann, consort of Henry, died Friday evening 19 February age 37. Recently of Portsmouth VA.   MORE 25 Feb 1836

SIRE, Mrs. Virginia, consort of Joseph, died 22nd inst at the home of her father Sylv. Labadie.   MORE 30 Sep 1828

SITES, Mrs. Martha, wife of John, died 9th inst.   COMB 17 June 1847

SKINNER, Mrs. Sarah, wife of Alfred, died last Saturday in St. Louis.   MORE 17 May 1827

SKINNER, Mrs. Eliza died in St. Louis 15th inst.   MORE 17 Jan 1834

SKINNER, Mary L. died age 18.   MORE 10 Oct 1835

SLACK, Elizabeth W., wife of John, formerly of Boone Co. MO, died 25th inst in her 48th year.   MORE 28 Jan 1847

SLOAN, Pocahontas, widow of Dr. S. C., died 14 Sept. (Estate record lists children as Mary A., Robert H., Samuel C. Jr., and Virginia.)   PWH 17 Sep 1845

SMITH, Eliza D., wife of Sanford J. Esq., died Yesterday. Funeral from St. George's Church.   SWERE 23 Apr 1849

SMITH, Mrs. Elizabeth T., wife of F. C., died 10th inst in her 23rd year. Native of KY.   LEXP 14 Jan 1845

SMITH, Mrs. J., wife of Joseph, died in Fayette.   MIN 24 Aug 1833

SMITH, Mrs. Joanna, wife of Judge S., died in Danville.   MIN 31 Aug 1833

SMITH, Mrs. -- wife of the late John B.N. died Sunday. (He died a few days earlier. Children: John B., Samuel, Henry, Sarah, Charles L., all under 21)   MORE 11 Sep 1822

SMITH, Miss Julia Ann, daughter of the late William Esq.,   MORE 12 Dec 1821
    merchant, died 6th inst. (SLINQ 12 Dec gives her
    mother's name as Eliza.)

SMITH, Mrs. Leona died 13th inst at her residence on the   JEFRE 17 Aug 1839
    Osage River in her 38th year. "Large family
    connection and 5 children."

SMITH, Mrs. Louise, wife of John, died Saturday last.   MORE 21 Feb 1832

SMITH, Lucy Ann, consort of Benjamin, died at the home   BOLT 11 Feb 1843
    of her father (not given) near this place Friday
    last. Funeral from residence of Simeon Switzler.
    Left an infant.

SMITH, Mrs. Mary, died 7th inst in her 78th year.   MORE 8 Jan 1849
    Residence 11th & Marion.

SMITH, Mary Eliza, wife of William Burwell and daughter   JINQ 27 Aug 1844
    of the late Thomas Goode, died 12th inst in her
    27th year. Formerly of Amelia VA.

SMITH, Mary M. died at the residence of her sister   MORE 1 July 1847
    Mrs. N. Marsh. Louisville and Maysville KY pc.

SMITH, Mary, oldest daughter of Major T. F. and Emilia   MORE 16 Oct 1837
    died at the residence of Mrs. Chouteau Friday
    evening last.

SMITH, Serena, late consort of Samuel, died 31 August   MORE 1 Nov 1836
    near Alexandria LA. (Her husband died 4 Sep.,
    noted "recently of Kentucky.")

SMITH, Mrs. Sarah G., consort of J. B., a merchant of   MORE 25 Oct 1831
    Potosi, died there 25 September.

SMITH, Mrs. Emilie A., wife of Major Thomas F. of St.   MORE 11 June 1842
    Louis, died at Cincinnati 4th inst. Buried
    from the residence of her mother, Mme. T. C.
    Chouteau, on Gratiot west of 7th St.

SMITH, Julia Ann, daughter of the late William, died   STCHMO 15 Dec 1821
    in St. Louis 6th inst.

SMITHERS, Mrs. Margaret, consort of Isaiah P. and   BORE 14 May 1844
    daughter of John S. and Elizabeth McFarland,
    died age 19y 9m 3d. Married 2½ years, her
    first child born 10 days ago.

SMIZER, Margaret, consort of George, died at Florissant   MORE 4 Nov 1845
    Sunday 2nd inst in her 27th year.

SOMERVILLE, Margaret, consort of John, died 8 January   PWH 14 Jan 1847
    age 59. Native of Clarksville, Harrison
                       Co., VA.

SOULARD, Miss Eliza C. died at the residence of her   MORE 4 Feb 1845
    brother Benjamin A. in her 38th year. Res.
    corner Hickory & 3rd. Catholic cemetery.

SOULARD, Mrs. Julia C., widow of Antoine, died in her   MORE 10 Mar 1845
    69th year. Resided 7th & Hickory. Interred
    Catholic cemetery.

SPARER, Catherine Ann, consort of John, formerly of   MORE 10 June 1845
    Baltimore, died of consumption 7th inst in her
    19th year. Baltimore pc.

SPARKS, Eliza Rebecca, daughter of John and Lavina, died   MORE 23 Feb 1847
    in Central Twp. 12 February age 13y 6d.

SPARR, Henrietta, youngest daughter of John H. and   MORE 30 Apr 1844
    Sarah A., died 29th inst at the Virginia
    Hotel. Presbyterian cemetery.

SPENCE, Mrs. Nancy died age about 85. Baptist for   MODE 15/13 Dec 1847
    30 or 40 years.

SPENCER, Emma M., wife of John A., died 1 November.   MORE 2 Nov 1847
    Resided Spruce between 5th & 6th.

STAPLES, Minerva, wife of John, died 2nd inst age 27.   CAMP 15 Dec 1848

STAPLES, Julia Ann, consort of William T., died   PWH 12 Mar 1842
    12 February. Left 4 children. Lynchburg pc.

STAPLETON, Mrs. Mary, consort of Harrison Esq., died   MODE 16/14 Dec 1846
    Sunday last.

STARK, Mrs. Hannah, consort of Capt. Horatio, the   MORE 17 Oct 1812
    present commander, died 22nd ult at
    Bellefontaine.

STARK, Mrs. Nancy Marshall, consort of Cyrus and   SPAD 17 Dec 1844
    daughter of Major A. Basye, died Monday last
    at Warsaw age 27.

STARNES, Virginia Goodare, wife of Capt. Nathan, died   SWERE 19 Nov 1848
    in Chicago 28 October age 24y 3m.

STEGAR, Mary, consort of Charles, died Sunday evening   MORE 25 Aug 1835
    last at the residence of Gen. Ashley, age 18.

STEVENS, Ann died at the residence of her son-in-law,   MORE 26 June 1849
    N. Paschall.

STEVENS, Mrs. John B. (with her husband, 10-year-old   MORE 10 Jan 1821
    son, and another small child) was murdered
    near Ste. Genevieve by John B. Duncan on
    13 December.

STEPHENS, Margaret, daughter of William of Dyer Co. TN   MORE 9 Dec 1843
    and granddaughter of Col. J. Trotter of St.
    Louis Co. died at the residence of Capt.
    Sparhawk. Methodist cemetery.

STETTINIUS, Helen, wife of Joseph of St. Louis, died   MORE 10 Sep 1841
    30th ult age 32 in Philadelphia.

STEWART, Mary, age 47, died at the residence of her   FULT 25 Aug 1848
    husband David in Lincoln Co. in early
    August. Member of the Christian Church.
    Left 7 children.

STEWART, Lucy, consort of Robert, died 19th inst.   PWH 20 Aug 1845

STICKNEY, Sarah Jane, consort of Benjamin, died age   MORE 21 Mar 1844
    27. Christ Church to Episcopal cemetery.

STILWELL, Charlotte T., consort of Edmund M., died 22nd ult.	BEA 9 Feb 1832
STIRMAN, Mrs. Paulina, widow of A. A. and daughter of Mrs. Fry (no date).	PWH 17 Sep 1846
STITES, Mary, widow of Edward, died "Thursday last" age 78. Baltimore pc.	MORE 12 Dec 1846
STONE, Fanny, wife of Capt. William, died 20th ult in Ralls County age 38.	PWH 8 Jan 1845
STORER, Harriet M., wife of Lieut. W. H., died in Baton Rouge LA on 10 April of consumption, in her 21st year.	MORE 18 May 1837
STORM, Mary J., consort of Henry T., died 9th inst.	MORE 13 Dec 1842
STOVALL, Mrs. Ann, consort of William P. (R?) died near Carrollton, Friday 10th inst, age 39.	BRUNS 21 Oct 1847
STRINGER, Mrs. Hannah died 30th ult "a stranger in a strange land." Funeral from her late residence over Mr. McGinnes' store on Market St. Philadelphia pc.	MORE 1 June 1842
STROTHER, Mrs. Elvira wife of Capt. Elijah J. died 9th inst age about 28.	BGRAD 16 Sep 1843
STROTHER, Mrs. Sarah G., wife of George F. Esq., died last Friday in St. Louis. (INP, quoting SLINQ, says she was in her 30th year, a native of Culpeper Co. VA, and daughter of the late Gen. Williams.)	MORE 10 May 1824
STROTHER, Caroline E., consort of Robert S., died 23rd inst age about 29. Methodist. (issue of 2 May states her funeral to be preached "tomorrow" by Rev. Dole at Mr. Baysie's.)	SALT 28 Mar 1840
STROUP, Hannah, wife of George, died in Cecil Co. MD 11th inst. Of St. Louis, formerly of Delaware.	MORE 28 Nov 1848
STUART, Ann, consort of W. H. H., died 1st inst at St. Mary's Landing age 22.	MORE 9 Mar 1846
STUART, Mrs. Jane C., wife of Judge Stuart of St. Louis Co., died 15 July age 40.	MORE 23 Aug 1824
STUDLEY, Mrs. Susan, consort of N., died Friday.	MORE 3 Aug 1830
SUBLETTE, Mrs. Isabelle, died "in this town" 21st inst.	STCHMO 24 Jan 1822
SUHRE, Sophia drowned off the Osprey 10th inst. Believed to have friends in Warrenton MO.	MORE 22 July 1846
SURRELL, Mrs. Ann died in Cape Girardeau 4th inst in her 54th year.	MORE 15 Aug 1846
SWON, Mrs. Ann K., consort of Capt. John C., died at her residence on 5th inst.	MORE 7 Aug 1832

TABB, Mary died at the residence of her brother-in-law John Riddle 23rd inst. Born in Jefferson Co. VA. Presbyterian. PWH 30 Sep 1843

TABOR, Mrs. Elizabeth, consort of C. M., died the morning of the 22nd. Left one son. Louisville Journal pc. MORE 29 Mar 1841

TACKET, Eliza, wife of Enoch and sister of Asa Wilgus, died at Rock Hill 6th inst in her 48th year. MORE 7 June 1849

TALBOT, Margaret L., consort of H. B., died 3rd inst in St. Charles of pulmonary disease. MORE 10 Apr 1835

TATE, Ann C., consort of Dr. Magnus W., died at Miami, Saline Co., in her 26th year. Charleston VA Free Press and Richmond Whig pc. MORE 13 Mar 1848

TATE, Mrs. Sophia W., consort of James, died 16th inst in Callaway. JINQ 26 Oct 1843

TAYLOR, Catherine, consort of J. B., died at Elm Spring Farm near Florissant in her 45th year, on 15th inst. Formerly of Baltimore and of Stafford Co. VA. MORE 19 & 22 Sep 1835

TAYLOR, Mrs. James died at her residence 9 miles south of St. Louis on 22 May. Formerly of Chester Co. PA; came to St. Louis County in 1815. MORE 27 May 1839

TAYLOR, Martha, daughter of William Esq., died 19th ult age about 18. WEM 1 Dec 1835

TAYLOR, Mrs. Mary H., consort of Henry of St. Louis, died in Carrollton IL 15th inst. MORE 19 July 1833

TAYLOR, Mary died at the residence of Mary Ann Wright. MORE 17 Aug 1837

TAYLOR, Mary Sheaff, wife of Moses and daughter of the late Philip Sheaff of Haverford Twp. PA died in her 78th year. Episcopal cemetery. MORE 3 Nov 1847

TAYLOR, Sarah, widow of Peter, died Tuesday last. SOV 18 Apr 1834

TAYLOR, Sarah J., consort of Thomas J., died 2nd inst at Pigeon, Grant Co., Wisconsin Territory. MORE 14 Aug 1843

TEMPLE, Mrs. __, consort of George, died Tuesday last on Yellow Creek. BRUNS 25 Nov 1848

TERRY, Mary E., wife of R. E. Esq. and daughter of the late Maj. John Hutchings of Pittsylvania Co. VA and Anna B. Hutchings, died 10th inst in her 24th year. Left 2 children, Henry about 4 and Kate about 2. Member St. Mary's Episcopal. MODE 14 Mar 1848

TESSIA, Ernestine, consort of J. Felix. (no other data) MORE 11 June 1849

THOMAS, Miss Amelia P. died of cholera. MORE 26 June 1849

THOMAS, Mrs. Elizabeth, wife of John of this city, died 4th inst. COMB 11 Feb 1847

THOMAS, Miss Helen M., daughter of the late Charles, died at Lexington MO 21st inst in her 20th year. MORE 5 Aug 1839

THOMAS, Mary Ann, consort of James S., died yesterday.	MORE 30 July 1835
THOMAS, Mrs. Mary, wife of Lieut. Charles, USA, died at the Arsenal near St. Louis Wednesday last.	MORE 7 Oct 1828
THOMAS, Mrs. Phenellah H., consort of Dr. L. C. of Roanoke, died 10th inst at the home of her father, Judge Head, in Randolph County.	BOLT 25 Sep 1841
THOMAS, Mrs. Sarah, consort of John P., died 24th inst age 44.	JINQ 31 Oct 1844
THOMPSON, Eliza, wife of William W., died yesterday after a long and protracted illness. (MORE 26 Sep gives death date as 25 September, age as 34, residence on Bellefontaine Road.)	SWERE 30 Sep 1844
THOMPSON, Mrs. Elizabeth T., consort of W. H., and daughter of the Rev. T. P. Green, died in Cape Girardeau 27 December.	BOLT 19 Mar 1842
THOMSON, Elvira C., consort of George, died 29 May. Left 2 small children.	MIN 30 May 1828
THOMPSON, Mrs. Hetty died 9th inst in Pittsburgh age 24.	MORE 17 Sep 1845
THOMSON, Mrs. Isabella, relict of the late Thomas Thompson, died near Philadelphia on 9 Dec. last in the 88th year of her age.	MORE 4 Jan 1831
THOMPSON, Mrs. Eliza B., relict of the late John W., died last Tuesday.	MORE 20 Apr 1826
THOMPSON, Mrs. Mary Jane died at Glasgow in her 33rd year.	BOLT 8 Feb 1845
THOMPSON, Mrs. Mary Katherine died Friday evening last. Age 56. Late of Memphis.	MOAR 27 Sep 1838
THORBURN, Isabella (or Arabella), wife of John, died age 23 years. Daughter of the Rev. A. Marshall decd., late of Edinburgh. Interred Presbyterian burying ground.	MORE 15 Jan 1840
TIFFIN, Mary Eliza, consort of Dr. Clayton, died in St. Louis yesterday.	SCOMB 20 May 1835
TILDEN, Lucy Ann, wife of John, died 18 August. (Her daughter Lucy Everett died 25 July.) Interesting note: in MORE on 2 Feb 1838, Jesse Pritchett warned the public against John Tilden, bigamist, who had married a lady in St. Louis but was found to have a wife and family in New York.	MORE 21 Aug 1838
TILDEN, Amelia, wife of John, died Saturday morning age 26. (Her daughter Lucy Amelia died the following March age 6m 26d.)	MORE 25 Nov 1843
TILFORD, Isabella A. died 14th inst age 23.	SLDU 18 Nov 1846
TIMON, Eleanor, wife of James, died last Monday age 62.	SOV 20 Apr 1833

TINSLEY, Martha Ann wife of W. H., died 27th inst. Her   BGRAD 30 Sep 1843
    husband died later in the same day and on the
    19th their infant Elizabeth Ann had died.
    They were lately from Virginia.

TISON, Mrs. Marie L. died Tuesday last.   MORE 22 Oct 1835

TITUS, Mary, wife of Dr. John W., died 11th inst.   MORE 12 Nov 1839
    Formerly of Rochester, NY. Funeral from
    residence of her mother, Mrs. Moulton, 39 Chestnut.

TODD, Jane W., wife of Albert Esq., died yesterday age   SWERE 14 Feb 1848
    29. (Her daughter Kate Wilson died 18 April age
    11m 6d.)

TODD, Mary Jane, second daughter of David, died Thursday.   MIN 18 Nov 1832

TOMPKINS, Mrs. Elizabeth, wife of the Hon. George D.,   JEFRE 27 Aug 1836
    died "this morning."

TOOLEY, Caroline V., wife of Clifton of Chariton Co.,   MODE 23 May 1848
    and daughter of George Cason Esq., died 4th
    inst near Glasgow. Baptist.

TOWN, Miss Eliza, daughter of Ephraim of St. Louis,   MORE 5 May 1834
    died in St. Charles 22nd ult.

TOWN, Mrs. Sarah, consort of Ephraim, died "a few   MORE 25 Aug 1836
    days since."

TOWNSEND, Mary Ann, age 16, died yesterday at the   SWERE 2 Sep 1844
    residence of her brother B. F. in St. Louis.
    Formerly of Pennsylvania.

TOZODE, Mrs. Mercy, wife of John, a merchant, died on   MORE 5 June 1832
    30 May.

TRACY, Mrs. Sarah, consort of Alfred, died Monday   MORE 2 July 1833
    morning in St. Louis.

TRACY, Mary E., sister of Alfred, died at Norwich CN.   MORE 24 Nov 1840

TRACY, Ann, wife of Edward Esq., died 20th inst in   MORE 21 June 1849
    her 45th year. Resided on 5th St. between
    Market and Wash. Louisville KY and Warwick CN pc.

TRASK, Lucy, wife of George died Saturday last. She   MORE 10 Jan 1842
    left a "large young family." Methodist cemetery.

TRASK, Selena, wife of George died 26th inst age 34.   MORE 27 May 1847

TRASKOSKI, Permelia V. died 10th inst. Funeral from   MORE 11 Jan 1849
    the residence of her husband on 16th St.
    between Franklin and Washington.

TRENT, Mrs. Mary, consort of Alexander, died 9th inst   BOLT 23 Sep 1843
    in Chariton County, age 41.

TRIGG, Docia, wife of Gen. Stephen, died Friday last.   MIN 7 May 1822

TRIPLETT, Mary, consort of William, died Tuesday 26   MORE 30 Apr 1841
    October age 49.

TUCKER, Mrs. Eliza D. died at Fulton MO 14th inst,   MORE 7 Apr 1829
    consort of Judge N. B. of St. George

71

TUCKER, Mrs. William, mother of C. L. of St. Louis, died in Boston Friday last.	MORE 20 Nov 1848
TUFTS, Sarah, wife of A., died in Collinsville IL on 5 October age 43.	MORE 11 Oct 1845
TUNSTALL, Mary P., wife of Warwick, died Friday last in St. Ferdinand in her 27th year. Left 3 children.	MORE 7 Dec 1847
TURNBULL, Mrs. Edward C. died in Frankford, Pike Co., on May 1st.	BGRAD 6 May 1843
TURNER, Mrs. Abigail, consort of Philip, died 23rd ult in her 76th year.	BOLT 7 Dec 1844
TURNER, Matilda, wife of Capt. A. W. and daughter of William Stone, died in Boone Co. 13 August.	MIN 19 Sep 1835
TURNER, Mrs. Sally, wife of Samuel, late of Beverly MA, died age 43 (48?). Boston and Salem pc. (SWERE gives name as Sarah)	MORE 27 Aug 1844
TURNER, Mary, consort of Thomasson, died 16th inst in her 80th year.	PWH 26 Apr 1849
TURNEY, Mrs. Hannah L., notice: she died Sept. 1843, place not stated; widow of Capt. Henry, a Revolutionary soldier; in her 108th year; believed to have a son in Missouri, a poor man, a cripple, thought to be "William."	MORE 13 Oct 1843
TWICHELL, Rebecca Burnet, wife of Timothy C. of New Orleans and daughter of the late Elizabeth Greene of Cincinnati. Funeral from residence of John F. Hunt on Collins St. to the Presbyterian burying ground.	MORE 9 Oct 1840
USHA, Eulalie, daughter of Domenico, died Saturday evening last of bilious fever near Carondelet, age 15.	MORE 10 Sep 1833
USHER, Mary, wife of the late Judge C., died in Chariton Co. in her 47th year. Philadelphia pc.	MORE 21 Apr 1847
VALLE, Rose, daughter of John B., died 26th ult in Fredericktown in her 19th year.	MORE 1 June 1848
VANBEBER, Mrs. Major died 22nd ult at the residence of her son-in-law N. B. in Green Co. MO. Age 104.	MORE 14 Aug 1838
VANDIVER, Nancy Ann, consort of Samuel, formerly of Hampshire Co. VA, died 9 September at her residence on Salt River in Shelby County. Left a large family.	PWH 25 Sep 1844
VAN DOREN, Sarah Ann, wife of William L., died 20 Oct.	MORE 21 Oct 1847
VAN DOREN, Susan H., wife of Rev. L. H., President of Columbia College, died in St. Louis on 10 January age 22.	MORE 12 Jan 1839

VAN HARTEN, Mrs. __ reported murdered at her home 10 or   MORE 25-6-7 Jan
     11 miles below Herculaneum, Jefferson Co.,   1841
     by three men. (But she was later reported
     to be recovering and the report of the whole
     matter seemed inconclusive.)

VANLANDINGHAM, Sarah Catherine, wife of Samuel, died   PWH 24 Sep 1846
     15th inst in her 24th year. Left 4
                     young children.

VAN METER, Mrs. Lucy M., consort of S. and daughter of   FULT 7 Dec 1849
     I. O. Hockaday, died in Clark Co. KY age 27.

VANSANT, Mrs. Virginia A., daughter of Mrs. Mary L.   MORE 11 Apr 1845
     Pastuer of St. Louis, died in New Orleans
     on 30 March age 21.

VAN ZANDT, Harriet Rosetta, adopted daughter of Dr.   MORE 27 Feb 1836
     Van Zandt, died Thursday last.

VASQUEZ, Amelia, widow of Antoine H., died 7th inst   MORE 10 Aug 1846
                     age 62.

VEITCH, Henrietta K., wife of Isaac McKendry Veitch,   MORE 28 May 1845
     died in her 17th year. Funeral from residence
     of her father, S. H. Herrick, 170 S. 6th.

VINCENT, Mrs. __ of Paynesville died in October.   BGRAD 9 Nov 1844

VON PHUL, Miss Maria, sister of Henry of St. Louis,   MORE 30 July 1823
     died last Monday in Edwardsville.

WADELL, Mrs. Nancy, wife of Maj. James W. of Lexington, LEXP 10 Sep 1844
     died yesterday evening age 53.

WADE, Abigail, wife of Isaac, died 26 September ae 38.   MORE 28 Sep 1844
     New York pc. (An infant daughter died 16 Nov.
                     age 1m 20 d.)

WALDEN, Mrs. Aylette died 4th inst in Monroe County,   PWH 21 Oct 1847
     leaving a husband and small children.

WALFORD, Ann, relict of the late Adam, died 17 March   SLINQ 22 Mar 1847
     age 75. Came to St. Louis in 1805; her
     husband died in 1815.

WALKER, Elvira, wife of John K. Esq., ex-sheriff,   MORE 23 July 1840
     died yesterday morning.

WALKER, Mrs. Elizabeth died at Commerce MO Thursday   MORE 9 Jan 1841
     afternoon in her 55th year; formerly of
     Wilmington, Delaware. Philadelphia pc.

WALKER, Sarah, relict of the Hon. John, died 12th ult   BRUNS 7 Apr 1849
     at Jefferson City. "Good neighbor and
     mother." Presbyterian.

WALLS, Alice Carr. (She was not quite 6 but the notice   WAR 28 Apr 1849
     reads that she was the only surviving child of
     C. E. Carr who had lost his wife and three
     babies in 18 months.)

73

WALLIS, Mrs. Sarah, wife of Lieut. E. Backus and eldest   MORE 22 Apr 1828
    daughter of Gen. Brady died 12 April at
    Jefferson Barracks in her 19th year. Born in
    Pennsylvania.

WALMSLEY, Mrs. Louisa, wife of James, died 5 November in   MORE 6 Nov 1846
    her 23rd year. (SLDU same date says 32nd
    year and adds "River papers please copy.")

WALSH, Mrs. Esther, age 75, died in this city at the   MORE 9 Jan 1840
    residence of her son-in-law (sic) Patrick
    Walsh. Resident 20 years. Funeral from 136 N.
    Main to Catholic cemetery.

WALSH, Mary Ann, eldest daughter of Patrick Esq.   MORE 11 Apr 1842
    Funeral from residence, 3rd & Plum.

WALSH, Mary Jane, member of the Sisters of Charity   MORE 20 Jan 1842
    for 29 years, died 9th inst in New Orleans.
    Native of Ireland, many years resident of
    Washington, latterly of New Orleans.

WALTERS, Mary Jane, daughter of C., died Thursday   SWERE 4 Nov 1844
    age 20.

WALTERS, Mrs. E., consort of F., died Saturday after   MORE 26 Nov 1839
    a short illness. Funeral from residence on
    Oak St., 1 door above Broadway.

WARD, Sarah Louisa, eldest daughter of Edward and   JEFRE 17 July 1841
    Mary S., died 16th inst in her 11th year.

WARE, Susan P., eldest daughter of William of near   BRUNS 27 Apr 1848
    Glasgow, died of scarlet fever 21st inst, age
    13 or 14.

WARFIELD, Margaret Ellen, wife of Charles and youngest   MORE 27 Sep 1841
    daughter of George Hammond, late of this
    city, died 14th inst. near Bloomfield,
    Iowa Territory. (Her daughter Margaret
    died 10 September 1842 age 11m 25d)

WARMSLEY, Mrs. Celina, consort of John, died 3rd   BGRAD 14 Oct 1843
    inst in Buffalo Twp. age about 43.

WARRANCE, Mary W., youngest daughter of William,   MORE 5 Oct 1838
    died Wednesday evening last age 15y 3m.
    Funeral from her father's residence, Mount
    Pleasant, to Presbyterian Burying Ground.

WARRANCE, Catherine Balsley, daughter of William, died   MORE 26 Oct 1841
    Sunday age 21 y 12 d. Funeral from residence
    in south St. Louis to Presbyterian
    Burying Ground.

WARRANCE, Catherine K., wife of William of St. Louis,   MORE 6 Sep 1847
    died at Gretna, opposite New Orleans, on
    23 August in her 61st year. Formerly of
    Philadelphia.

WASERMAN, Elizabeth, wife of Jacob, formerly of   MIN 28 Aug 1821
    Augusta Co. VA, died Monday last.

WASH, Mrs. Frances, consort of Hon. Robert of St. Louis County, died at Pensacola where she had gone for her health. Interred in St. Louis County.	MORE 20 Jan 1829
WATERS, Nancy M., wife of Dr. Thomas, died in Bowling Green 24th inst age 31.	BGRAD 30 Mar 1844
WATHAN, Mrs. Julia, consort of Dr. Richard M. and daughter of Agnes Smith, died 14th inst.	PWH 19 July 1843
WATKINS, Julia Glover died at the residence of Col. John South Tuesday, age 17.	BGRAD 23 Sep 1843
WATSON, Mrs. Ann, widow of James of London, died at the home of her daughter Mrs. Fleischman 16th inst age 76. Resident of US 22 years.	MORE 17 Mar 1846
WATTS, Martha of Howard Co. died 23 June at Ft. Laramie. Left husband and 2 children.	MORE 7 Oct 1850
WATTS, Mrs. Sarah, wife of Benjamin, died 7th inst. Left "husband and friends."	BOLT 14 Aug 1841
WAUGH, Lise E., consort of James, died, date not shown. Resided 12th & Pine. Catholic cemetery.	MORE 27 June 1849
WEISEMAN, Catherine, native of Germany, died 14th inst age 18.	MORE 18 Jan 1845
WELCH, Julia died 9th inst. Funeral from residence of her husband, 6th & Green.	MORE 10 Apr 1849
WELCH, Mrs. Mary of St. Louis died yesterday.	MORE 23 Aug 1839
WELLS, Sarah, consort of George N. of Lincoln Co., died at the residence of Joseph Roberts in Pike Co. 28 January.	BGDB 1 Feb 1845
WELLS, Mrs. Mary, formerly of Jefferson Co. New York, died in St. Louis Wednesday age 41.	SLINQ 15 Aug 1847
WELLS, Mrs. Mary, consort of Richard of Gravois settlement, died 23rd inst age 44. Left a large family of children.	MORE 26 Oct 1839
WELLS, Mrs. Mary, consort of Joseph Sr., died at Gravois age 73. Emigrated with her husband in early days, from Pennsylvania to Kentucky.	MORE 1 Jan 1841
WELLS, Harriet Amanda, wife of R. W., died 3rd inst age 24. Left 3 children.	JEFRE 8 Feb 1834
WELLS, Mary, wife of Nicholas, died 3 February in Louisville, Lincoln County. (Her husband age 60 died 11 February.) Both natives of KY. Settled in Missouri 28 years ago. Methodist.	BGRAD 17 Feb 1844
WELLS, Cynthia, wife of Nicholas B., died in Cuivre Twp. 4 November.	BGRAD 9 Nov 1844
WELLS, Susan R., daughter of Samuel, died 15 February of typhus at the home of Mrs. Heald in St. Charles County. Age 16.	MORE 3 Mar 1842

WENDOVER, Harriet, wife of Joseph R., died 5th inst   MORE 7 Sep 1847
   age 23. Funeral from St. Paul's Church to
   Episcopal Cemetery. (Her daughter Harriet
   Amma died 3 weeks later age 8 weeks 3 days.)

WESCOTT, Mrs. Catherine D., wife of Maj. Robert, died at   MORE 11 Dec 1832
   Potosi 26th inst in her 45th year, leaving
   a large family -- "children mostly young
                              and helpless."

WESCOTT, Miss Theodosia N. died 29th ult at Potosi.   MORE 14 Apr 1834
   Formerly of Philadelphia.

WEST, Mary Virginia, wife of James M., died 5th inst.   CAMP 15 Dec 1848

WETMORE, Mrs. Sarah Jane, consort of Diogenes, died   MORE 15 June 1841
   yesterday morning age 22. Left 2 children.
   (Her son Hume died a month later age 1y 11d.)

WETMORE, Jane Ann died at Grand Pass, Saline Co., on   MORE 14 May 1844
   2nd May of "dropsy of the head." Consort of
   George C., formerly of Montgomery Co.

WHALEY, Mrs. William died Monday last leaving 6   PWH 4 Jan 1840
   small children.

WHARTON, Eliza F., wife of W.Y., Surgeon US Army and   MORE 14 Aug 1848
   daughter of the late Mahlon Ford died
                              13th inst.

WHEELER, Johanna died 9th inst after an illness of   MORE 24 Jan 1832
   20 hours, at Marthasville. (Her husband
   died the same day after an illness of 37
   hours. His name was Capt. Chester.)

WHEELER, Elizabeth, consort of John of Manchester,   MORE 2 June 1845
   died yesterday at the residence of
                              John M. Wimer.

WHEELER, Ellen M., wife of David, died yesterday   MORE 3 Apr 1844
   age 34. Resided Olive between 3rd & 4th.

WHELEN, Harriet M., wife of Henry Esq., died at the   MORE 10 May 1842
   residence of her mother in Easton, PA on
                              25 April.

WHERRY, Mrs. G. H., consort of Joseph A., late   MORE 29 Nov 1843
   Register of the City of St. Louis, died at
   her residence in the county Monday last.

WHISTLER, Mrs., wife of Maj. John, died last Sunday   MORE 6 Apr 1826
   at Cantonment Bellefontaine.

WHITE, Mrs. Barthena B., consort of George W., died   JEFRE 18 Nov 1843
   Sunday last age 29. (Her few-days-old infant
   also died.) Member Christian Church.
   (JINQ 16 Nov. gives husband as J. W., postmaster at Jefferson City.)

WHITE, Mildred, consort of Capt. John, died 23rd inst   BRUNS 28 Apr 1849
   in Howard Co. age 59. Methodist.

WHITE, Nancy died 17th inst in her 49th year. Formerly   MORE 18 Mar 1848
    Brownsville PA. Funeral from the residence of
    James H. White, Morgan & 15th Sts. Brockville IA
    and Wheeling VA pc.

WHITE, Susanna, consort of Isham died 20 April.   PWH 23 Apr 1842

WHITE, Mrs. William H., mother of Keith and Edward,   MORE 29 July 1846
    died 27th inst in her 29th year.

WHITING, Ellen Maria Nickerson, youngest daughter of   WAR 3 Mar 1849
    Marcus and Eunice N., died Monday last in
    her tenth year.

WHITTENBURGH, Rachel, widow of the late John, died 2nd   INP 24 Apr 1824
    inst age 74. Daughter of Thomas Mason of
    Virginia, where she was born and reared.
    Resided here 23 years, died at the home
    of her daughter.

WIGGINS, Mrs. Cornelia, wife of Samuel, died 6th inst   MORE 6 Mar 1845
    in Cincinnati.

WILCOXSON, Sarah Margaret, daughter of Joseph M. and   BOLT 31 Dec 1842
    Amanda Ann, died 25th inst.

WILD, Sarah Ann, wife of J. C., died 8 January. Funeral   MORE 10 Jan 1842
    from the home of her father William Humphreys,
    corner Franklin & 12th.

WILGUS, Elizabeth Jane, wife of James, died in St. Louis   MORE 26 Jan 1846
    yesterday. Interred Presbyterian cemetery.

WILGUS, Sarah, relict of James died (date not shown).   MORE 10 Aug 1838

WILKERSON, Jane, wife of Thomas P. and daughter of E. B.   BRUNS 27 Jan 1849
    Cabell, died at her father's residence
    near Keytesville 21st inst in her 25th year.
    "Wife, daughter, mother."

WILKINSON, Mrs. Emelie, died in Perry Co. 8th inst   MORE 16 Apr 1849
    in her 55th year.

WILKINSON, Letitia Ann, wife of N. E., died 13th inst   MORE 16 Aug 1847
    age 19. Formerly of Cincinnati.

WILLIAMS, Mrs. Elizabeth, relict of the late Col. Sam,   MIN 19 July 1834
    died in Chariton Co. 10 July.

WILLIAMS, Mrs. Elizabeth died at the residence of her   MORE 30 June 1835
    son-in-law John Bingham near St. Louise
    Sunday, age 67.

WILLIAMS, Elizabeth died at the residence of her son-   MORE 18 Jan 1848
    in-law John Hall 17th inst age 89.

WILLIAMS, Louisa, consort of Graham, died in Clark Co.   PWH 6 Aug 1846
    29 July.

WILLIAMS, Mrs. Judith F., wife of John R., died at her   LEXP 25 Mar 1845
    residence in Ray Co. Saturday 15 March in
    her 49th year. Formerly of Prince Edward
    Co. Virginia.

WILLIAMS, Mrs. Mary Ann, consort of George Washington, died 28th ult in her 20th year. Funeral from residence of her father, Nathan H. Stevenson, on 21 November.	BOLT 18 Oct 1845 " 15 Nov "
WILLIAMS, Mary B., wife of Robert P., died age 55. Funeral from St. Paul's Church.	MORE 19 Aug 1844
WILLIAMS, Ann, wife of Col. H. T., died in Chariton Thursday last. Daughter of Thomas and Ann Graves of Orange Co., Virginia. In her 23rd year; married 29 May, 1827.	MIN 12 Oct 1827 " 19 Oct "
WILLIAMS, Sarah, wife of James and daughter of the late Richard Mitchell, all of Washington Co., died in her 17th year after a long illness. Formerly of Allen Co., KY.	MORE 13 Sep 1842
WILLIAMS, Mrs. Mary Jane, died 7th inst in Randolph Co. in her 21st year. (Her husband Sebastian died 5 days later in his 39th year. They left 3 small children.)	MODE 22 Sep 1847
WILLOCK, Ann Eliza, daughter of Capt. David, died of cholera at Palmyra 16 June. (possible wife; see Bowen, Mary Mildred)	JEFRE 18 July 1835
WILSON, Ann Maria, consort of Robert died 9 Dec. ae 21.	SWERE 10 Dec 1848
WILSON, Clara E., wife of John C., died 12 January age 20 years. Residence #3 Washington Ave.	MORE 13 Jan 1847
WILSON, Harriet Melvina, wife of George, died 12th inst. Cincinnati & Covington KY pc.	MORE 14 Feb 1849
WILSON, Ellen, consort of the late James of Philadelphia, died 16 August in her 72nd year.	MORE 17 Aug 1847
WILSON, Johanna, died 2nd inst "upwards of 80." Refers to son George. Resided 3rd St. between Spruce & Poplar. Episcopal cemetery.	MORE 30 Oct 1845
WILSON, Mary, consort of Ephraim, died 10th inst. Presbyterian. (A daughter of Ephraim, Mary, about 10, died 6 March. PWH 15 March.)	PWH 12 July 1849
WILSON, Miss Martha died Saturday in her 18th year.	STGAZ 13 Nov 1846
WILT, Mrs. Christian, daughter of Maj. George Wilson, died 12th inst.	MORE 14 Dec 1816
WILT, Miss Juliana died 27 September at the home of Stephen Hempstead near St. Louis. Daughter of Abraham of Philadelphia.	MORE 11 Oct 1824
WINDHAM, Miss -- (and her father) brutally murdered. They were shot and axed and their house set afire. Mr. Windham lived long enough to describe the assailant.	MORE 25 Nov 1834
WINES, Mrs. ___ died 14th inst an an advanced age.	PWH 26 Aug 1847
WING, Eliza, consort of Frederick died 30 November in Troy.	BGRAD 7 Dec 1844

WING, Adaline, died in St. Louis 7 February age 32.   SWERE 15 Feb 1847
Formerly of Livermore, Maine.

WISELEY, Margaret B. died in her 28th year and Rachel S.   BOLT 14 Sep 1844
died in her 25th year. (Margaret on 3 September
and Rachel on 4 September). At residence of
their father, name not given.

WITZELL, Mrs. Mary, consort of William Y., died Wednesday   MORE 12 Apr 1831
last in St. Louis.

WOLFORT, Miss Minerva died Friday last age 13 years.   MORE 7 Sep 1830

WOODS, Elizabeth, daughter of Sarshel of Carroll Co.,
died 15 December at the residence of J. L. Tracy   COMB 31 Dec 1846
in Boonville where she was attending school.
She was 16 years old.

WOODRUFF, Mary A., wife of James P., died 12th inst in   BGRAD 3 Feb 1844
her 34th year.

WOODWARD, Frances died yesterday, a native of Nottaway   MORE 7 Feb 1844
Co. VA. Funeral from residence of her son
Elbert Esq. on Morgan St. Petersburg VA pc.

WOODWARD, Laura, daughter of Elbert "followed her mother   MORE 24 Jan 1844
to the grave." (She was 2y and 5m old.)

WOODSWORTH, Mrs. Mellisa L., wife of H. D., died in her   INJN 12 Sep 1844
28th year in Independence, leaving
"children."

WORKMAN, Mary, wife of David, died 30th ult in Franklin.   MIN 12 Oct 1826

WRIGHT, Mary of Taney Co. died 22 June at the South   MORE 7 Oct 1850
Platte Crossing, age 35.

WRIGHT, Mary Elizabeth, relict of Dr. John C., died   PWH 14 & 28 Dec
2nd inst age about 27.   1848

WRIGHT, Mary Ann, widow of the late Maj. Thomas, died   MORE 6 Jan 1846
5th inst age 48.

WRIGHT, Mary Elizabeth, eldest daughter of John and   MORE 13 Sep 1847
Jemima L. Owen and wife of Erie Wright, died
12 September in her 20th year. Louisville,
Cincinnati and New York pc.

WRIGHT, Martha Tatum, wife of James A., died 19th ult   MORE 10 Feb 1844
in Philadelphia age 29.

WRIGHT, Thrace Caroline, wife of James G., died 4th inst   PWH 15 Jan 1846
in her 35th year. Left 7 children.

WRIGHT, Mrs. William of Pena Twp. died 18th ult.   SALT 5 June 1841

WYATT, Anna Catherine, consort of John, died at Camp   MORE 3 Sep 1850
Branch, Warren Co. 24 August age 33y 2m 12d.
Eldest daughter of William Thomas of Kent Co.
MD. Left 4 small children.

WYGANT, Catherine Emily, wife of (illegible) died   MORE 8 Apr 1849
7th inst ae 31. (SWERE says wife of M.)

YEATS, Mrs. Jane died in St. Louis Co. Wednesday 23rd ult in her 58th year.	MORE 15 Aug 1834
YATES, Mary Malinda died Thursday 7th inst age 17.	MORE 11 Aug 1845
YEATMAN, Angelica Charlotte, consort of James E. Esq. and daughter of Col. J. P. Thompson died yesterday. Baltimore, Alexandria, and Nashville pc.	SWERE 14 May 1849
YELDER, Mrs. (and her husband) were killed by a negro belonging to the estate of Philip Coontz (Coonce) near Herculaneum. Yelder was a "Dutch" shoemaker. Their year-old infant was slightly hurt.	MORE 7 Mar 1844
YEOMAN, Marion, wife of William, died (no date). Residence 14th and Orange.	MORE 23 June 1849
YOUNG, Sydney Ann, daughter of David B., died in New London 14th inst. Formerly of Bath Co. Kentucky. Age 34.	PWH 21 Nov 1840
YOUNG, Sophia, consort of Col. Jesse, died Thuesday. Rhoda Ann, daughter of Jesse, late of Zanesville, OH died Sunday of consumption. Frances, daughter of Jesse, died 5th inst age 19. Methodist Sunday School teacher.	MORE 12 Sep 1835 " 22 Nov 1833 " 13 July 1838
YOUNG, Lucretia, consort of Joseph L. and daughter of Archibald Williams decd of Carter Co. TN died in Bolivar, Polk Co. 15 November age 30 y 9m 6d. Methodist. 5 children.	SPAD 21 Nov 1846
YOUNG, Theodocia, consort of the late A.H., died in St. Louis yesterday in her 60th year. Formerly of Fayette Co. Kentucky.	MORE 26 Sep 1845
ZIMMERMAN, Mrs. Zuelma, wife of James M., died at Troy, Lincoln Co. Left "children."	MORE 28 Aug 1838

ABRAMS, Mary Ann w/William H., of bilious fever Sunday evening ae 62. Louisville, Baltimore pc.   MORE 12 April 1853

ADAMS, Martha Ann w/Eli (ruling elder, Cumberland Presbyterian Church) on 6 April. She was born in Missouri 26 February, 1820.   BOBS 6 May 1851

ADAMS, Talitha, w/Smith, formerly of Caldwell Co., in Texas 5 February.   STGAZ 29 March 1854

ALLEN, Diana consort of Thomas in her 40th year. She was formerly of Augusta Co., VA, nee Snapp, left three children including a son John who died a few days after her, age 19m 3d. Husband's initials given as T. R. (Obit MORE 14 August)   MORE 18 & 29 July, 1851

ALLEN, Phoebe Ann consort of Robert L. and d/Nathaniel Pendleton of Pendleton Co. VA, in Warren Co. (8 November?) ae 33.   MORE 8 Dec 1851

AMENT, Mrs. Judith D., formerly of Canton, mother of Joseph P. Ament of Palmyra, 12 July in Nashville TN.   CANE 3 Aug 1854

AMICK, Elizabeth w/Leander 23 March.   GLWT 3 Apr 1851

AMONETT, Mrs. Hannah of Cooper Co. in Texas a Oct.   LEXP 3 Oct 1854

AMOS, Adella D. in her 9th year. Funeral from residence of her aunt, Mrs. Douthitt.   MORE 24 Nov 1851

ANDERSON, Mrs. Juliet, of consumption, in Hillsboro.   MORE 15 March 1851

ANDERSON, Mrs. Maria J. late consort of Dr. S. H., on 29 September. Funeral from residence of P. A. Saul, interment Baptist cemetery.   HANT 30 Sep 1852

ASHBROOK, Frances T., w/Henry Jr., 13 June. Funeral from residence of her father-in-law, Levi.   MORE 14 June 1851

BALDWIN, Pauline Amanda dau/Capt. John and Amanda F. (Trallen), yesterday, age 12.   MORE 4 June 1852

BALDWIN, Sarah Ann, w/Smith, 21 January.   MORE 22 Jan 1851

BANNON, Jane Fitzgerald, consort of Henry, 30 April in her 28th year.   MORE 1 May 1853

BARADA, Mrs. Elizabeth, at the residence of Isidore Barada in Buchanan Co. 27 March in her 77th year.   MORE 9 April 1853

BARBEE, Cornelia Kingsberry, w/Rev. S. J. M., in Brunswick 23 July.   GLWT 31 July 1851

BARNARD, Margaretta consort of John H., 2 April in her 37th year.   MORE 3 April 1851

BARNARD, Sarah; "friends of the Rollin Clark family" invited to her funeral, Congregational Church. Vermont pc.   MORE 7 June 1853

BARNES, Mrs. Anne, age 71.   LEXP 25 Jan 1854

BARNETT, Ruth, w/M. of Callaway Co., 1 May age 41.　　MORE 10 May 1852

BARRY, Julia w/Edward at the residence of her son-in-　　MORE 28 July 1851
law George Buchanan in her 62nd year.
Philadelphia pc.

BEEBE, Cornelia Kingsbury (see BARBEE), w/Rev. J. J. M.,
pastor of the Brunswick Presbyterian Church.　　MORE 1 Aug 1851
Born in Clyde, New York; age 27.

BELL, Hannah M., w/James M., in her 37th year.　　BOBS 6 May 1851
Richmond VA pc.

BENSON, Mary Jane, d/Edon and Celia, in Portland,
Callaway Co. 25 December age 29y 10m 3d.　　MORE 4 March 1852

BENTON, Prudence, d/D. and Susanna, 8 July　　MORE 14 July 1853
age 15y 8m 25d.

BERRY, Susan, consort of Dr. Daniel, 3 July in her
67th year. Native of Massachusetts.　　MORE 4 July 1851
Interred Bellefontaine Cem.

BERTHOLD, Eliza, relict of Nicholas, 12 September in
her 63d year. Funeral Church of the Messiah.　　MORE 12 Sep 1853

BIRCH, Bettie T., consort of James H., 1 March in
Plattsburg in her 22nd year. Lexington and
Frankfort KY pc.　　STGAZ 9 March 1853

BIRCH, Sarah Catherine consort of John suddenly in
Prairie Park, Clinton Co., Thursday last in
her 45th year.　　MORE 7 June 1852

BIRKENBINE, Mrs. Caroline, relict of the late John,
"this morning" age 34.　　MORE 26 Nov 1851

BISCH, Mary, w/Charles of Ste. Genevieve, at her
father's plantation near Napoleon, Arkansas
on 27 March.　　MORE 12 April 1853

BISHOP, Mrs. Elizabeth w/DeWitt C., M.D., 16 January
age 33, leaving 3 children. Chicago pc.　　STGAZ 21 Jan 1852

BLACKFORD, Mrs. M. of Boone Co. 24 June at Fort
Laramie, of cholera, age 50.　　MORE 7 Oct 1850

BLAKEY, Amanda w/John D. and d/A. Huntsberry of
Lexington, MO in Central Twp., St. Louis Co.,
age 26y 4m 4d.　　MORE 24 June 1850

BLANCHARD, Ameriana(?) Vasquez, w/E., ae 32.　　MORE 11 March 1852

BLUE, Rebecca, consort of Richard, 16 October in
Trenton in her 68th year.　　WEPT 18 Oct 1851

BOGGS, Abigail, consort of Robert, in Howard Co.
30 April ae 50y 2m 15d.　　MORE 10 May 1852

BONE, Mrs. ___, w/Judge J.P., at Clinton 12 April.　　OSIN 16 April 1853

BORROWMAN, Louisa consort of David, 22 March　　MORE 25 March 1853
ae 22y 17d. Nashville pc.

BOURKE, Ann d/Patrick 18 July. Interred Catholic cem.   MORE 19 July 1851

BOYLE, Mrs. Ann, formerly of Mt. Jackson, Shenandoah
    Co. Virginia, 15 February ae (52?).   MORE 17 Feb 1851

BOYLE, Tabitha consort of C., 29 September age 34.
    Interred St. Vincent's Cem.   MORE 30 Sep 1851

BRADFORD, A. M. w/Adolphus, 28 March in her 31st year.
    She resided at Collins & Ashley.   MORE 29 March 1853

BRADFORD, Eliza, age 49. Funeral from the residence
    of her son, A. Bradford.   MORE 16 July 1851.

BRADFORD, Mary E., 2nd daughter of Major R. B. of
    Johnson Co., age 8, killed by lightning.   KCEN 19 July 1856

BRADLEY, Frances, of Howard Co., of cholera 21 June
    at Scott's Bluff, age 23.   MORE 7 Oct 1850

BRADLEY, Mary E., of Liberty, 2 June.   STGAZ 8 June 1853

BRANHAM, Mary w/Manlius and d/Moses Prewitt, in
    Columbia 28 March.   MORE 1 April 1851

BRANNAN, Eliza relict of Hugh at her residence in
    Gravois, 10 February, in her 65th year.   MORE 11 Feb 1852

BRAY, Mary E., w/W. A. and d/Col. James Young, while
    aboard a steamboat with her husband and children,
    returning from California, 9 July.   LEXP 26 July 1854

BREEDING, Rosetta w/C. P. in Parkville, Platte Co.,
    8 December. Methodist. Eight children.   MORE 6 Jan 1853

BRIDGE, Maria A., relict of Harrison P., in her 28th
    year. Funeral from the residence of her
    brother-in-law, Hudson Bridge, to the Church
    of the Messiah. Interred Bellefontaine Cem.   MORE 27 April 1853

BRIGGS, Darcus, w/Caleb, in St. Joseph 19 August.   MORE 5 Sep 1850

BRIGGS, Miss Mary W. in her 21st year. Funeral from
    the residence of Benjamin Fowler.   MORE 12 July 1851

BROOK, Mrs. Eleanor Ann 14 February in her 82nd year.
    Covington KY pc.   MORE 15 Feb 1852

BROTHERTON, Aurelia d/Marshall and Elizabeth, 27 March   MORE 28 March 1853
    age 6y 10m 5d. Resided Broadway and
    Chambers.

BROWN, Susan Elizabeth d/Robert, in Jackson (Cape
    Girardeau Co.) 26 December ae 11y 1d.   MORE 19 Jan 1853

BURT, Laura A. w/William 12 May ae 41.   MORE 14 May 1853

BUTLER, Rebecca consort of Linzy and d/E. & C. Bowen
    5 February in her 28th year, leaving
    three children.   STGAZ 9 Feb 1853

BUTTER, Catherine 15 January in Hickory Co. in her
    26th year, leaving husband and four children.
    Formerly of Harrisburg, PA. Toledo and
    Wooster OH pc.   MORE 24 Feb 1853

CALLAHAN, Mrs. Beston, of Warren Co., murdered 22 May
    by a negro boy belonging to her family.   GLWT 29 May 1851

CALLISON, Dicy consort of Robert, 12 July ae 50y 4m.
    She was a Baptist.   GLWT 17 July 1851

CARROLL, Mrs. Patrick, 10 May in her 40th year.   MORE 11 May 1853

CASSADY, Mrs. M., of Henry Co., 19 June age 45,
    of diarrhoea.   MORE 7 Oct 1850

CATHERWOOD, Angelina C., oldest daughter of Robert H.,
    in her (20th? blurred) year, 9 September.   MORE 10 Sep 1851

CHARLESS, Sarah relict of Joseph, yesterday, in her
    81st year.   MORE 4 March 1852

CHAUVIN, Marie Louise, relict of Jacques, yesterday
    (78th? 76th?) year.   MORE 22 Feb 1852

CHILDS, Eliza T., consort of Nathaniel Jr., yesterday
    in her 43rd year. Interred Wesleyan cem.   MORE 21 Aug 1851

CLARK, Abby Churchill w/Meriwether Lewis, 14 January
    ae 34y 10m 5d.   MORE 15 Jan 1852

CLARK, Mrs. Mary ae 71y 6m 7d.   MORE 20 Aug 1853

CLEMENS, Eliza, wife of James, 20 August.   MORE 22 Aug 1853

CLEMENS, Pamelia, widow of the late Judge, in
    Hannibal.   MORE 27 Sep 1851

CLOUGH, Sarah Elizabeth, age 20, formerly of
    Montville, Maine, at the residence of
    J. R. Clough.   MORE 14 Feb 1853

COLE, Anne M., w/Henry, 15 August in Bridgeton
    in her 27th year.   MORE 25 Aug 1853

COLLINS, Mrs. Caroline, w/John, d/R. and Nancy
    Burnett, in Holt Co. 9 January ae 22y 9m.
    Left two children.   STGAZ 26 Jan 1853

CONNELLY, Mrs. Elizabeth, d/Mrs. Elizabeth Kiger,
    age 21.   MORE 10 May 1851

COOLEY, Mary w/M. C., 4 April ae 23(?)y 5m.
    Funeral, residence of Mr. Aldrich.   MORE 6 April 1851

CORDELL, Fanny, d/late John, in Jackson 4 January.   MORE 19 Jan 1853

COTTON, Elizabeth M., w/Rev. Joseph, at the home of
    her father, Henry Pritchett, 22 September
    in Warren Co.   MORE 26 Sep 1851

CRANE, Emily C. w/J. W. 28 July in her 30th year.
    Louisville pc.   MORE 29 July 1851

CRARY, Mary, 20 January of consumption ae 54y 6m.
    Mother-in-law of Joseph E. Ward (or Ware).   MORE 22 Jan 1851

CREASY, Elizabeth relict of Thomas, at an advanced
    age.   LEXP 1 and 8 Feb 1854

CRENSHAW, Martha C., consort of Anthony W., 11 May in her 53rd year. Nee Brandford, native of Cumberland Co., VA.	STGAZ 18 May 1853
CURRY, Mary, consort of George, in Cape Girardeau 2 March ae 45. Left a large family.	MORE 8 March 1853
CUTTING, Harriet Louise d/Amos and Theodora, 7 July. Boston pc.	MORE 11 July 1853
DAVIS, Jane Elleanor, d/Dr. D. L. and Mary E., in Canton 29 June age 13.	CANE 6 July 1854
DAVIS, Helen A. w/Charles at the residence of her father Judge Cooper in Fredericktown 2 July age 22.	MORE 10 July 1851
DAVIS, Alice, wife of the late John of Maryland, 9 September.	LEXP 13 Sep 1854
DAVIS, Sarah Ann of Caldwell Co., 24 June at Castle Bluff of cholera, age 19.	MORE 7 Oct 1850
DeMUN, Clara, d/Julius and Isabella, 4 April in her 19th year.	MORE 5 July 1853
DEROUIN, Marie, age 68, 29 April at Mrs. Chauvin's.	MORE 30 April 1853
DILLON, Lucy, 24 October ae 61. Funeral from home of her son-in-law J. W. Paulding.	MORE 25 Oct 1851
DOBYNS, Mrs. Anne, w/Major E., Wednesday ae 50. Funeral from 2nd Baptist Church. Maysville KY and Lexington MO pc.	MORE 7 Feb 1852
DOUGLASS, Jane M., wife of the late S. Howard of St. Charles, 15 May.	MORE 17 May 1852
DOUGLAS, Mrs. Jane, w/William A., in St. Joseph 10 March in her 38th year.	STGAZ 16 Mar 1853
DOWDING, Sarah Jane d/John of Harrisburg, Pennsylvania, 11 February. Funeral from the residence of R. S. Elliott.	MORE 12 Feb 1851
DRAKE, Alice Ingram w/George T., Thursday. Interred Bellefontaine Cem.	MORE 4 March 1852
DREW, Sarah, relict of C., formerly of Maine. Age (63? blurred). Interred Episcopal Cem.	MORE 16 Feb 1851
DRUMMOND, Ann Thena, d/Sarah, in her 18th year.	LEXP 28 June 1854
DUNCAN, Elizabeth, consort of Samuel of Fayette, 23 May.	MORE 10 May 1852
DUNCAN, Nancy sister of James in Boone Co. 1 May age 26.	STGAZ 1 June 1853
DUNHAM, Semira w/George and d/Samuel Steel 26 April in Callaway Co. age 24.	MORE 10 May 1852
DUNN, Mrs. Martha of St. Louis 13 June near Ash Hollow, age 19.	MORE 7 Oct 1850
DUNSMORE, Mrs. Frances in her 85th year. Funeral from residence of son-in-law John Whitehill.	MORE 17 June 1853

EARNEST, Pamelia Ann d/Barton L. in Carroll Co. 18 July age 18. She was a Methodist. Nashville Christian Advocate pc. — BRUNS 16 Aug 1849

EASTON, Abial w/Rufus in St. Charles, 22 February. — MORE 23 Feb 1849

EDDY, Frances E. d/George and Catherine, 7 May. — MORE 8 May 1853

ELLET, Mary Letitia only d/John in her 17th year. — MORE 6 July 1851

ELY, Mrs. Nancy Artemetia, 1 June ae 19y 9m. Interred Bellefontaine Cem. — MORE 2 June 1853

EPPERSON, Mary w/Charles and d/Benjamin and Julia Threlkeld, 29 May. Formerly of Boone Co. — STGAZ 1 June 1853

FAIRLAY, Mary A. w/Matthew yesterday ae (35?). — MORE 3 June 1852

FARRAR, Caroline Matilda Garland w/Dr. John O. in her 21st year, yesterday. Funeral from Christ Church. — MORE 2 Sep 1851

FASSITT, Margaret Barclay, w/Alfred and d/John A. Barclay, 31 July. Interred Philadelphia. — MORE 1 Aug 1851

FERBER, Sarah E., consort of William K. and d/Joseph Gash, in Clay Co. 21 April in her 26th year. — MORE 10 May 1851

FICHTENKAM, Isabella, d/George and Elizabeth, 29 March ae 7y 5m 25d. Resided 7th & Marion. — MORE 20 March 1853

FINE, Mrs. Ann, in her 83rd year. Funeral from the residence of her son Carter. — MORE 22 May 1853

FIELDS, Elizabeth, of Harrison Co., at Chimney Rock 16 June of cholera, age 17. — MORE 7 Oct 1850

FISHER, Mrs. S. M., consort of Robert, 24 September age 31. — MORE 25 Sep 1851

FISHER, Theresia w/Henry, 16 August. — MORE 17 Aug 1851

FLINN, Maria M. in Greensville, Wayne Co., 1 March. Consort of L. H. Flinn. — MORE 11 March 1852

FONTAINE, Malinda w/Thomas of Batesville, Ark. and d/Robert G. Watson of New Madrid, 21 April in her 40th year. — MORE 13 May 1853

FRAME, Elizabeth, consort of Archibald, 18 August ae 29y 5m. Louisville and Cincinnati pc. Interred Bellefontaine Cem. — MORE 19 Aug 1851

FRAME, Mary, w/James of Brunswick, in Glasgow 16 May. — GLWT 26 May 1852?

FREES, Lydia Maria, consort of Peter W. and eldest d/Peter W. Johnston, 11 February. — MORE 13 Feb 1853

FULLER, Margaret, w/Orlando and d/Mrs. Mary McLaughlin, formerly of Nashville, 17 March. — MORE 19 March 1851

GAMAGE, Mrs. Ruhamah, 22 June ae 29. Boston pc. — MORE 24 June 1852

GAMEREIL, Lucy S., youngest d/James and Mary E., 5 August ae 6y 9m 20d. — MORE 6 Aug 1853

GARDNER, Susan D. w/Robert, age 37. A Baptist, left   OSIN 10/30/1852
    five children.

GARRISON, Mrs., wife of the late William C., of   WAR 5/12/1853
    consumption.

GILBREATH, Sarah Ann, w/Rev. John N., of typhoid   MORE 19 Nov 1851
    at Des Peres 8 November, age 24.

GILLIAM, Mary T. consort of William T. 11 September   GLWT 18 Sep 1851
    in Saline Co. age 39.

GILSON, Elmira Amanda w/George (a printer) 7 July   MORE 9 July 1853
    age 22.

GLASSFORD, Elizabeth w/Samuel M., age 23.   MORE 6 July 1851

GLENRY, Mary Elizabeth, eldest d/Joseph and Phoebe,   MORE 14 May 1853
    13 May ae 20y 11m 15d. Funeral from
    Second Baptist Church.

GORMAN, Elizabeth w/John at Hartville, Wright Co.,   MORE 11 Sep 1851
    31 August ae 27.

GORMAN, Margaret, consort of Joseph E. and d/Pierce   MORE 1 Aug 1851
    Grace, 31 July in her 33rd year.

GRATIOT, Victoria Ann, d/J. P. B., in Arkansas   MORE 16 Sep 1853
    23 August age (16? blurred).

GRAVES, Elizabeth M. consort of ? M? Saturday   LEXP 15 Feb 1854
    morning last.

GREEN, Isabella relict of Joel H. in Fayette 24 March.   GLWT 3 April 1851

GUDGEL, Laura M., late of Utica, at the Lexington   LEXP 5 July 1854
    Female Seminary.

HACKNEY, Mrs. Mary age (21? 41? blurred)   MORE 14 Apr 1851

HALL, Mary Jane, consort of David, in Florissant   MORE 4 April 1851
    2 April.

HANCOCK, Lucinda, w/Dr. J., 15 May.   MORE 16 May 1853

HANCOCK, Mrs. Louisa, late consort of Austin, in this   HANT 30 Sep 1852
    county, of flux, age 34.

HARLOW, Olive A., age 15, at the residence of her   MORE 25 March 1851
    brother (B or R). Bangor ME pc.

HARMON, Mary widow of Thomas, 30 June in her 45th   MORE 1 July 1851
    year. Interred Rock Spring Cem.

HARRISON, Margaret, consort of William P. and d/George   MORE 29 Feb 1852
    Morton of St. Louis, in Hannibal.

HARRISON, Mary, 16 November age 58.   MORE 17 Nov 1851

HARSHAW, Zaida Ann, d/Zaida Ann and William H.,   MORE 15 Feb 1853
    14 February age about 4.

HART, Victoria Shelby, d/David and Sarah, formerly   MORE 9 Oct 1851
    of Fayette Co. KY, now of Buchanan Co. MO. No
    date or age.

HAYES, Eliza w/J. L. H. and d/John Largy, 30 August   MORE 31 Aug 1853
    ae 32y 11m 13d. Funeral from the Cathedral
    to St. Vincent's Cem.

HAYWOOD, Mrs. Mary, 26 June in her 62nd year.   MORE 28 June 1852

HEAPS, Rebecca w/William at her home in St. Louis Co.   MORE 8 Feb 1852
    2 February. Formerly of Barford Co. Maryland.

HEATHERLY, Dina V. of Jasper Co. at Ash Hollow   MORE 7 Oct 1850
    25 June age 12.

HECK, Charlotte age 26. Funeral from the residence   MORE 21 April 1853
    of her brother Bremen, Rocky Branch,
    Bellefontaine St.

HENDERSON, Kate McCulloh, d/George and Mary, 9 July.   MORE 10 July 1851

HERNDON, Maria L., consort of Dr. James H. of Randolph   GLWT 6 Feb 1851
    Co. and d/James D. Taylor in Cincinnati   MORE 29 Jan 1851
    23 December in her 21st year.

HICKMAN, Mrs. Agnes at her home on Bellefontaine   MORE 2 Sep 1851
    Road 29 August in her 60th year.

HINDS, Mrs. E., consort of Capt. John, 1 January   MORE 4 Jan 1853
    ae 17y 5m. Louisville, Wheeling, Peoria pc.   " 8 Jan "
    (Later gives name as Amanda)

HORAN, All--er, consort of Robert, 1 July age 43.   MORE 2 July 1851
    Interred Rock Spring Cem. (Her daughter Mary   " 17 "
    Eleanor died two weeks later ae 8 m) NY pc

HORRELL, Ann, relict of Rev. Thomas, 18 November in   MORE 20 Nov 1851
    her 64th year. Native of Prince Georges Co.
    Maryland. Funeral from St. George's Church.

HUGHES, Mary, consort of Col. Z. C. of Howard Co.,   GLWT 12 June 1851
    7 June.

HUGHES, Mary Ann, consort of John R., yesterday in her   MORE 22 Sep 1851
    31st year. Interred Bellefontaine Cem.

HUGHES, Mrs. Sarah in Platte Co. 24 May, ae ca 60.   GLWT 19 June 1851

HULETT, Zerelda, consort of William and d/William and   STGAZ 3 Aug 1853
    Elizabeth Phillips, 25 July in Rocheport
    age 18.

HUSSEY, Loretta, youngest child of Mr. and Mrs. B.,   MORE 16 July 1851
    formerly of Holton, Maine. Ae 3y 20d.

JACOBY, Caroline w/Frederick, 11 August in her   MORE 12 Aug 1851
    27th year. Interred Bellefontaine Cem.

JAMISON, Meeky w/David, 31 December ae 49y 9m 12d.   MORE 1 Jan 1853
    Interred Wesleyan Cem. Nashville pc.

JANE, Elizabeth relict of William (a Revolutionary   MORE 26 Apr 1852
    soldier) in Jackson Co. at an advanced age.
    Native of North Carolina.

JARRETT, Cordelia, d/the late Mrs. Malvine Smith,   MORE 13 Aug 1851
    Monday evening.

JEFFRESS, Mary N. w/E. B. and d/R. R. Gregory, in Franklin Co. 1 September age 23.	MORE 7 Sep 1853
JESSE, Louisa w/Judge Robert 8 January age 35.	STGAZ 21 Jan 1852
JOHNSON, Mrs. Malinda D., consort of Stephen, near Platte City in her 27th year. Native of Boonville, d/Robert P. Clark.	MORE 22 Aug 1851
JONES, Agnes W., consort of Augustus, in Potosi 15 January in her 57th year.	MORE 22 Jan 1853
JOY, Hannah F., w/Benjamin and d/the late Thomas Dinsmore of Conway NH, 1 January in her 52nd year.	MORE 4 Jan 1854
KELLY, Mrs. Mary, consort of John W., at Oregon, Holt Co., 6 November ae 51. Born in Greenbriar, Virginia in 1800, to Missouri in 1840. Left husband, one daughter, three sons.	SASE 15 Nov 1851 " 22 "
KEMPER, Laura, d/Simeon and Jane, 4 September.	STGAZ 14 Sep 1853
KENNEDY, Jane w/Dr. John in Central Twp. 7 July in her 59th year.	MORE 9 July 1853
KERCHEVAL, Elizabeth M., 12 March in St. Joseph in her 18th year.	STGAZ 17 March 1852
KERR, Mrs. Mary Ann, relict of George. Funeral from the Christian Chapel.	MORE 23 May 1851
KINTZ, Margaret, consort of Francis, of cholera 25 June. Harper's Ferry pc.	MORE 27 June 1851
KIRKHAM, Ann M. w/David of St. Louis at the home of her mother in Montgomery Co. 25 June in her 27th year.	MORE 29 June 1852
KREEN, Cornelia w/Frederick, 1 December.	MORE 2 Dec 1851
KRING, Sarah A. w/John N. and d/Lewis Crigler in Fayette 10 September.	GLWT 11 Sep 1851
KUBLER, Louise w/C. C. 2 December in her 46th year. Mobile pc.	MORE 3 Dec 1851
LADY, Harriet w/John, 6 April in her 27th year. Resided 6th St., south of Pine.	MORE 7 April 1853
LANHAM, Mrs. Semphronia at her home in St. Louis Co. 5 November in her 74th year; late of Prince Georges Co. Maryland.	MORE 24 Nov 1851
LATHAM, Lydia Ann age 32, d/Major John Slack of Boone Co., 20 May. Presbyterian.	STGAZ 8 June 1853
LATOUR, Mary Jane d/Peter and Odilia, 29 May ae 17y 6m. Her family lived on Manchester Road. Interred Rock Spring Cem.	MORE 30 May 1852
LEAHEY, Mary, mother of Timothy, a native of Ireland, 15 May age 72. Interred Rock Spring Cem.	MORE 16 May 1853

LEHMANN, Hannah, consort of Joseph, 16 October ae 49. GLWT 23 Oct 1851

LETCHER, Evalina consort of William H. and d/the late MORE 2 Sep 1851
    Ambrose Ranson of Franklin Co. in her 22nd year.

LEWIS, Mary Ann w/James A. W. 23 March ae 23. MORE 26 Mar 1853
    Lynchburg VA pc.

LITTLE, Miss Ann 7 September ae 40. Cincinnati pc. MORE 9 Sep 1853

LIVERMORE, Elizabeth Douglas w/Emory, 7 October. STGAZ 12 Oct 1853

LIVINGSTON, Nancy E. consort of Thomas and d/James MORE 19 Aug 1853
    Gibson of Lincoln Co. at Richwoods,
    Washington Co., 9 August.

LOGAN, Rosannah W., consort of John, in Perryville STEGPD 22 Jan 1853
    24 December in her 63d year. Kentucky pc.

LOYD, Mrs. E., w/Jerry, near Canton 15 November. CANE 23 Nov 1854

LURTON, Cynthia, d/Charlton and Cynthia, age STCWR 3 June 1854
    12y 5m.

LYONS, Mrs. Eliza Jane, youngest daughter of the late MORE 19 May 1852
    Nathaniel Childs Sr. of St. Louis, in
    Madison, Indiana. Interred St. Louis.

McALISTER, Mary Harriet, youngest daughter of the late MORE 6 March 1851
    Rev. Alex. Interred Wesleyan.

McCLEY, Mary w/Capt., in Glasgow 8 May ae 22. MORE 10 May 1853
    Interred St. Louis.

McENTIRE, Margaret, relict of John, "Wednesday" in her MORE 13 Feb 1852
    (56th?) year. Interred Rock Spring Cem.

MacKENZIE, Mary Marshall, d/Kenneth, 23 January. MORE 25 Jan 1853
    Funeral from Christ Church.

McKNIGHT, Mary A., widow of James, 25 March in her MORE 28 Mar 1853
    66th year. Virginia pc.

McLAUGHLIN, Cora, w/P. L., 13 May. STGAZ 18 May 1853

McLEAN, Hannah of St. Louis near Edwardsville 2 Sept. MORE 6 Sep 1851
    of inflammation of the brain, age 17.

McMAHON, Rosa 7 January in her 18th year. MORE 11 Jan 1851

McMANUS, Maria in her 40th year. Funeral from home of MORE 26 April 1853
    her brother. Interred Bellefontaine Cem.

McNULTY, Mary Ann of Chariton Co., 24 June en route MORE 7 Oct 1850
    west, age 14.

MAGEE, daughters of C. R. and Sarah R. of Monticello: CANE 5 Jan 1854
    Lucinda ae 8y 4m 8d on 23 December; Louisa Ann
    ae 3y 3m 13d on 29 December.

MANSFIELD, Jane age 67 at the crossing of the South MORE 7 Oct 1850
    Platte, 18 June.

MANSFIELD, Elizabeth of Chariton Co. at Ash Hollow MORE 7 Oct 1850
    1 July age (38?). Left husband, family.

MARVIN, Mary, oldest daughter of Major A. C., in Clinton, Henry Co., 26 February.	MORE 11 March 1853
MASSIE, Mrs. A. D./w/Henry A. in Boonville 21 June.	MORE 27 June 1850
MASSEY, Sarah, widow of Samuel, in Jefferson Co. 10 July age 62.	MORE 23 July 1851
MEAD, Elizabeth w/Col. George and d/John Francis Renou of Salem, Massachusetts, 26 June age 42.	MORE 27 June 1852
MEGARY, Miss ___ of St. Joseph, en route west.	MORE 7 Oct 1850
MERRITT, Melissa, w/Jesse, in Perry Co. 25 June at the home of Dr. Reuben Shelby. Lynchburg pc.	MORE 19 July 1851
MILLER, Ann Harrison 9 May at the home of L. H. Calvert in her 22nd year.	MORE 11 May 1853
MILLER, Anna F. w/Thomas and d/Hugh and Anna Wardlaw of St. Louis in Hannibal 23 June in her 28th year.	MORE 8 July 1853
MILLER, Mrs. Martha, w/James, in St. Louis Co. 25 February.	MORE 26 Feb 1852
MONROE, Mrs. ___, w/Rev. Andrew, near Hydesburg in Ralls Co. 26 August.	CANE 1 Sep 1853
MUNROE, Jerusha, relict of William, in her 61st year. One of the earliest settlers.	GLWT 26 June 1851
MOORE, Mrs. Rebecca, consort of John, 28 April at Old Chariton.	GLWT 1 May 1851
MORRIS, Mary w/Henry 22 August in her 36th year.	MORE 23 Aug 1851
MORTON, Mary w/Dr. Thomas M. at their residence on Gravois Road 6 January. Maysville KY pc.	MORE 8 Jan 1851
MOSELEY, Martha B., w/Harry Jr., in Boonville. Native of Pittsfield, Mass. Wife, mother.	BOBS 25 March 1851
MURPHY, Elizabeth w/John in Saline Co. 1 September in her 50th year.	GLWT 11 Sep 1851
MURPHEY, Margaret w/Dennis, 17 June.	MORE 18 June 1853
MEYER, Mrs. Hannah, widow of P. A., mother of J. C., at the home of her son-in-law F. V. Hackman on 16 November.	MORE 19 Nov 1851
NEEPER, Mary A., consort of Joseph, Monday evening. Left husband and little children.	WAR 12 Apr 1853
NELSON, Emily, consort of William P., 30 September in her 35th year.	MORE 1 Oct 1851
NISBET, Mary Goode w/Robert and d/John and Mary Lemoine of Petersburg, Virginia 7 January in her 25th year.	MORE 8 Jan 1853
OLCOTT, Marie Louise, d/Charles and Marie, 5 May ae 13y 5m.	MORE 6 May 1852

ORME, Sarah Jane West, only d/Robert and Matilda, age 5y 2m 8d. Fulton MO, Rochester NY pc. — MORE 20 Sep 1851

OVES, Miss Harriet. Funeral from home of Samuel Sheree. Interred Bellefontaine Cem. — MORE 5 June 1853

PAGE, Mary, consort of J. D., 24 April in her 27th year. Interred Wesleyan Cem. — MORE 26 April 1852

PARSONS, Mary, consort of Capt. M. M. and d/R. W. Wells, in Jefferson City 8 July. — MORE 13 July 1853

PECK, Rosina Hinclay, d/E. S. and R. C., late of St. Louis, in Marysville CA 7 July in her 8th year. — MORE 18 Sep 1850

PENN, Louisa, eldest daughter of the late Shadrach Jr. Interred Wesleyan Cem. — MORE 11 June 1851

PHELAN, Ellenor, consort of Michael, 28 February age 26. Interred Rock Spring Cem. — MORE 1 March 1851

PHILIBERT, Harriet w/Adolph age (39?) at their residence, 5th and Franklin. — MORE 23 June 1852

PILKINGTON, Margaret, d/Henry, in her 19th year. Interred Wesleyan Cem. — MORE 25 April 1853

PITCHER, Ellen M., w/Henry, age 24. — MORE 1 Feb 1851

POSTON, Martha, w/Richard, in St. Francois Co. 18 May. — MORE 28 May 1851

POTTS, Mrs. Lucy Jane "a few days short of 29 years of age" at Boonville 10 February. Left husband and five children. — BOBS 24 Feb 1851

POWERS, Catherine, widow of William, yesterday. — MORE 17 June 1852

PRATT, daughters of Col. Warner of Edina, Knox Co.:
Amma Hill 14 Aug ae 5y 16d — CANE 25 Aug 1853
Ellen 13 Aug ae 1y 9m 9d — " 23 Aug 1854

PREWITT, Ella T. d/Moss of Columbia in New Orleans 6 February in her 19th year. — GLWT 20 Feb 1851

PUTNAM, Harriet A. w/H., 8 May ae 32. Boston pc. — MORE 10 May 1851

RECTOR, Lydia, widow of Thomas, 21 March age 53. Catholic ceremony. — MORE 22 March 1853

REILLY, Eliza consort of Patrick, 30 June age 32. — MORE 1 July 1851

RENARD, Marie Louise Papin, widow of Hyacinthe, 16 September in her 69th year. — MORE 17 Sep 1853

RENSHAW, Augusta A., youngest d/William, 31 August age 19. — MORE 1 Sep 1853

REYBURN, Alicia w/Thomas G., formerly of Baltimore, in her 62nd year. — MORE 9 Aug 1851

RICHARDSON, Elizabeth, widow of William, mother of William K. of St. Joseph, 3 September in St. Joseph. (STGAZ 31 Aug gives date of death as 27 August.) — MORE 11 Sep 1853

RICHART, Jane Creigh, w/A. L., 17 September age 29y 3m 3d; Jane Connell, their daughter, 13 September age 1y 6m 19d.   CANE 22 Sep 1853

RICKETTS, Elizabeth, a student at the Convent in Ste. Genevieve.   MORE 29 July 1851

RIDDLE, Jane, Esther (age 24) and ___ age 18, all of Pike Co., in June at the crossing of the South Platte.   MORE 7 Oct 1850

RILEY, Narcissa w/Dr. Henry W. in Hartsville, Wright Co., in her 29th year.   MORE 17 Aug 1851

RINEHART, Mary Magdeline, consort of Benjamin, 9 January in her 38th year. Reading PA pc.   MORE 10 Jan 1852

RINGELING, Lizzie, only d/Francis and Ellen, age 5y 10m.   MORE 19 Sep 1853

ROBB, Mary Houston, w/Charles, 18 May in her 42nd year. Interred Bellefontaine Cem. Lexington VA pc.   MORE 19 May 1853

ROBINSON, Malvina w/J. R. Jr., 1 January. Baltimore and Cincinnati pc.   MORE 3 Jan 1851

ROBINSON, Virginia Augusta d/William and C. A., age 5y 6m. Resided Main and Pine.   MORE 5 Aug 1854

ROCHEBLAVE, Mrs. Maria Louisa age 79. Funeral from residence of Michael Cerre. Interred Rock Spring Cem.   MORE 4 April 1853

ROGERS, Catherine consort of Francis, 20 September age 25. Interred Rock Spring Cem.   MORE 21 Sep 1851

ROUSSIN, Clementine, d/Etienne, 28 January in Richwoods, Washington Co., age 30.   MORE 5 Feb 1853

ROUSSIN, Aspasie, consort of Etienne, at Richwoods 14 September age 39.   MORE 20 Sep 1851

ROUTH, Ann, widow of Calvin, 27 August. Natchez and New Orleans pc.   MORE 29 Aug 1851

RUNYON, Kitty, eldest d/B. H. and Mary R., age 6y 10m. Nashville pc.   MORE 13 Jan 1851

RUTHERFORD, Mrs. H. L. in Huntsville 7 October.   GLWT 9 Oct 1851

RYAN, Mrs. Elizabeth 18 February in her 60th year. Native of Queens Co. Ireland. NY & CA pc.   MORE 21 Feb 1853

RYAN, daughters of Thomas and Anna: Mary Louisa 18 April ae 4y 1m 13d Fanny Eugenia 24 April ae 3y. Interred St. Vincent's Cem.   MORE 19 and 25 April 1853

SAGNER, Lois Evadne d/Albert and Emeline age 4 years. Emeline w/A. R. age 35. Nee Hecker.   MORE 14 June 1852

SALING, Mrs. James, 16 August at an advanced age.   GLWT 21 Aug 1851

SAMUELS, Mrs. Adeline consort of Dr. G. G. and d/Mann   HANT 19 Aug 1852
    Butler in St. Louis 15 August.

SCHOENTHALER, Amanda, eldest d/Godfrey and Mary,   MORE 25 April 1853
    20 April ae 11y 2m.

SCHROEDER, Henrietta Virginia, w/Rev. W. H. of   MORE 3 Sep 1850
    Clinton, Henry Co., 11 August. Late of
    Richmond, Virginia.

SCOTT, Mrs. ___ of Cape Girardeau at Fort Laramie   MORE 7 Oct 1850
    26 June.

SCUDDER, Mrs. Julia. Philadelphia pc.   MORE 25 Feb 1851

SCUDDER, Mrs. Mary, widow of Dr. Charles, 23 June   MORE 24 June 1852
    age 48. Maysville KY pc.

SEAMAN, Martha, formerly of Clark Co., in Nevada   MORE 18 Jan 1852
    20 November age 16y 10m.

SETTLE, Matilda w/Thomas, sister of Marshall   MORE 31 Jan 1853
    Brotherton, at her home on St. Charles Road
    about 11 miles from St. Louis. Interred
    Bellefontaine Cem.

SHACKELFORD, Mrs. Eliza last Sunday morning in   GLWT 13 March 1851
    Saline Co. in her 53rd year.

SHANNON, Marian d/John and Eleanor 26 January   MORE 29 Jan 1853
    age 17y 8m 10d.

SHARP, Isabella, formerly of Girard Co., New York,   MORE 10 May 1852
    at the home of her uncle, William Adams, in
    Howard Co. 27 April age 21.

SHAVER, Jane, consort of Rev. F. L. B., in   GLWT 16 Oct 1851
    Lexington 30 September.

SHAW, Martha, a native of Wales, at her home in   MORE 8 Sep 1853
    St. Louis age 71. Methodist for 25 years.

SHAW, Susan D., consort of H., 18 February in her   MORE 10 March 1853
    53rd year in Shelbyville. A Methodist.

SHEARER, Mrs. Elizabeth w/Sextus at the home of   MORE 22 Jan 1853
    Mrs. Christophs, age 51.

SHELTON, Mary Emeline, consort of Pines H. and   MORE 22 June 1851
    d/Capt. John Wyatt of Warren Co., 8 June
    in her 26th year.

SHEPLEY, Louisa w/John H. 17 January in her 25th   MORE 18 Jan 1852
    year. Funeral from the home of Mrs.
    George Collier.

SHERMAN, Mrs. Elnora C., mother-in-law of Dr.   STGAZ 14 Sep 1853
    Ringo, 11 September.

SHIN, Nancy, consort of Joel, in Grundy Co.   WEPT 25 Oct 1851
    12 October age 70.

SHREVE, Florence, youngest d/H. M. and Lydia,   MORE 10 Jan 1851
    8 January age 18m.

SHUGANT, Elizabeth, w/Eddam, on the road from Iowa to Texas. MORE 26 June 1852

SIMMONDS, Mary V. of Franklin Co. 15 June on the upper crossing of the South Platte, age 2½y. MORE 7 Oct 1850

SIMMONS, Mary Ann d/Moses and Leah, of typhoid, 3 February age 8y 6d. STGAZ 9 Feb 1853

SIMONDS, Theresa w/Captain John and sister of Henry Geyer, 6 August age 50. MORE 7 Aug 1851

SITTON, Harriet E., consort of Judge William M., in Andrew Co. 20 November. SASE 22 Nov 1851

SKINNER, Ann, widow of Curtis, at the home of her son-in-law in her 65th year. Funeral from the residence of T. Polk, 9th Street between Morgan and Franklin. MORE 30 March 1853

SLACK, Mrs. Electa Ann, oldest daughter of Capt. William Thayer of St. Louis, in New Orleans. MORE 19 Aug 1853

SLATER, Sarah Burrell, consort of B., 8 September age 31. MORE 11 Sep 1851

SLEMENS, Mary Thomas, only d/Mrs. Garrard, Thursday last in Hannibal age 17. HANJ 28 Oct 1852

SMITH, Evelyne w/Christopher in Crawford Co. 4 May. MORE 15 May 1851

SMITH, Elizabeth, consort of Joseph B., 24 August age 35y 9m 1d. STGAZ 31 Aug 1853

SMITH, Ann W., consort of Zenas, in Greenville, Wayne Co., 7 June. MORE 26 June 1851

SNOW, Sally Etoline, consort of Dr. Charles V., at Irish Grove, Atchison Co., 7 October age 24y 26d. Formerly of Vermont, late of Montrose Iowa. STGAZ 10 Nov 1852

SPARKS, Mary consort of Aquilla, 25 June. MORE 26 June 1851

SPORE, Mrs. Nancy w/Daniel 21 May in her 51st year. Rising Sun, Iowa pc. MORE 22 May 1853

SPRECHER, Caroline w/Ph. J. of consumption, age 26. MORE 9 March 1851

SPRINKEL, Mrs. Emma Jane, consort of Alex, in Hannibal 26 July. HANT 27 July 1852

STAVELY, Mrs. Catherine, consort of John W., in South Hannibal 30 July age 28y 12d. A Methodist, d/Barton and Elizabeth Ingraham. HANT 31 July and 12 Aug 1852

STEVENS, Clarissa L., widow of Simeon, 10 February age 41. Funeral, Unitarian Church. MORE 11 Feb 1852

STILES, Mrs. Margaret in Weston, Platte Co., 27 August in her (30th or 39th?) year. MORE 6 Sep 1851

STREETS, Lorinda, consort of Robert, 20 September in her 39th year. Funeral from the home of the late Judge Walton, on St. Charles Road. Interred family burying ground. — MORE 21 Sep 1851

STRINGER, Mary Hager, w/Thomas and d/Samuel Hager of Newburgh, New York, 12 May. — MORE 27 May 1852

SUMMERS, Mary w/Michael, 7 January age 37. — MORE 8 Jan 1852

SWACKHAMMER, Mrs. ___, w/A. J., of Monroe Co. and formerly of Glasgow, 27 October. — GLWT 18 Nov 1852

TAFFE, Mrs. Bridget, 9 July in her 61st year. — MORE 11 July 1853

TALBOT, Mrs. Frances, w/John M. of Cooper Co. Formerly of Bourbon Co., Kentucky. Member of the Church of Jesus Christ, or Reformers. Left husband and children. — BOBS 29 April 1851

TAYLOR, Mrs. Ellen M., 16 October. She resided on Mullanphy near Broadway. — MORE 17 Oct 1851

TAYLOR, Mrs. Catherine, w/G., in Ste. Genevieve 15 June age 67. — MORE 24 June 1852

THOMAS, Mary, relict of John, of Simpson Co. Kentucky at the residence of James G. Smith in Mercer Co. She was born in King and Queen Co., Virginia in 1749, thus aged 102, and had been a Methodist for 60 years. — WEPT 11 Oct 1851

THOMPSON, Mrs. Sarah, in Grundy Co. 8 October ae 49. — WEPT 18 Oct 1851

TIERNEY, ___, w/Anthony, 14 June. Funeral from St. Patrick's Church. — MORE 15 June 1853

TOLSON, Mary, consort of Capt. William and d/Jefferson Ray, in her 29th year. — MORE 10 May 1852

TOPLIFF, Mrs. A. M. in St. Joseph 11 August, age about 60. — MORE 19 Aug 1851

TRUSSELL, Elizabeth w/Frederick on the road from from Iowa to Texas. — MORE 26 June 1852

TUCKER, Mary G. W. w/Charles L. 8 September ae 36. Funeral from the Church of the Messiah. Interred Bellefontaine Cem. — MORE 9 Sep 1853

TUNSTALL, Frances Jane, youngest d/Thomas and Mary, age 5y 9m 2d. — MORE 12 Nov 1851

TURNER, Mary Jane w/William C. 21 April ae 25y 24d. Providence RI pc. — MORE 24 April 1851

TURNER, Rebecca w/Edmund in her 37th year. — MORE 13 Aug 1853

TURPIN, Jane w/William, formerly of Lafayette Co., in Oregon 3 November. — STGAZ 29 March 1854

TUTT, Julia, consort of William J. and d/John P. and Sally A. Martin, formerly of Kentucky, near Versailles (MO) 29 September, ae *ca* 21. — MORE 1 Oct 1851

TYLER, Adeline, consort of Dr. Benjamin, 1 April of consumption. Interred in the family burial ground, St. Louis Co. Richmond VA pc. — MORE 2 April 1851

Mary A. only child of Benjamin R. at the residence of Capt. William Tyler. Richmond VA pc. — MORE 15 May 1851

VANBURGH, Eleanor, consort of Cornelius, formerly of New York. — MORE 13 July 1851

VAN HORN, Elizabeth, w/C. M., 5 January. — MORE 6 Jan 1853

VOWLES, Mrs. Annie, at the residence of her son Newton Vowles, Oak Grove, near Warrenton, age 100y 9d. — BOBS 15 April 1851

WADDELL, Elizabeth, consort of William, 1 April in Lexington in her 31st year. — MORE 26 April 1852

WADE, Ann, w/Samuel, 3 August in Buchanan Co. ae 35. — STGAZ 11 Aug 1852

WALKER, Mary J. w/Rev. Joseph 24 May ae 33. Funeral from 2nd Baptist Church. — MORE 25 May 1853

WASSIN, Miss Marian Wallace at Palmyra Sunday last. — HANT 9 Sep 1852

WATSON, Sarah w/Wesley in St. Louis Co. 18 February in her 34th year, leaving six children. — MORE 23 Feb 1851

WATTS, Martha of Howard Co. 23 June at Fort Laramie. Left husband, two children. — MORE 7 Oct 1850

WEAKLEY, Margaret, formerly of Shelby Co. Kentucky, 20 August at the home of William McGrew. — STGAZ 31 Aug 1853

WEBSTER, Mrs. Joanna in Clarksville 14 July in her 73rd year. — MORE 17 July 1851

WELLER, Mrs. H. C., widow of Rev. George and mother of Rev. Richard H. Weller of Missouri, in Vicksburg 13 January. — MORE 26 Jan 1853

WELLS, Mrs. Mary, at the residence of James McCausland on 9 August ae (36 or 56). Louisville pc. — MORE 13 Aug 1853

WHITE, Eliza, consort of C. F., 25 September in her 37th year. — MORE 26 Sep 1851

WHITE, Clara B. d/Robert and Isabella, 9 March ae 3y 10m 2d. Wheeling pc. — MORE 16 March 1853

WHITEHEAD, Anna Eliza d/James R. and Jane G., 19 July ae 1y 29 d. — STGAZ 27 July 1853

Martha Ann oldest daughter of James W. 24 November ae 15y 10m 5d. — STGAZ 21 Dec 1853

WHITTAKER, Ann w/Francis 4 May age 37, leaving seven children. Interred Bellefontaine Cem. — MORE 6 May 1852

WILLIAMS, Nancy Jane, consort of Benjamin, 17 January in her 74th year. — GLWT 23 Jan 1851

WILLIAMS, Harriet L., 12 August at the home of John Cozine ae 22y 11m. — STGAZ 10 Aug 1853

WILLIAMS, Mrs. Malinda, consort of John, formerly of Livingston Co., in California 21 November in her 42nd year.   MORE 8 Jan 1853

WILSON, Sarah B. d/Mrs. Mary, age 16. She resided on Collins nr Biddle.   MORE 18 Oct 1851

WIMER, Catherine Elizabeth d/George A. and Elizabeth 13 May age 13. Funeral, St. Xavier.   MORE 14 May 1853

WOOD, Martha Jane d/G. F. and Martha Jane, yesterday age 3y 7m 26d.   MORE 13 Feb 1853

WOODS, Mrs. Rebecca at the home of her husband in Marion Co.   MORE 29 June 1851

WRIGHT, Mary of Taney Co. 22 June at the South Platte Crossing, age 35.   MORE 7 Oct 1850

    Nancy of Taney County at the South Platte Crossing 22 June, age 8.

WYATT, Anne Catherine, consort of John, 24 August at Camp Branch, Warren Co. ae 33y 2m 12d, leaving four small children. D/William Thomas of Kent Co., Maryland.   MORE 3 Sep 1850

YEATS, Elizabeth w/Thomas D. in Bonhomme Twp., St. Louis Co., age 43y 5m.   MORE 13 Oct 1851

YORE, Mrs. Margaret, 9 December ae <u>ca</u> 58. Interred Catholic Cem.   MORE 10 Dec 1851

YOUNG, Julia Y. Perry w/John H. 6 October ae 22.   MORE 9 Oct 1851

ZIEGLER, Mrs. Luzia w/Sebastian 30 December in her 61st year. Rochester NY and Carlisle PA pc.   STGEPD 8 Jan 1853

+ + +

www.ingramcontent.com/pod-product-compliance
Lightning Source LLC
Chambersburg PA
CBHW031426290426
44110CB00011B/540